Praise for Ac

"*Accidental Monk* prompted the deepest kind of reflection for me.... By engaging Wil's story, I discovered my own story at a deeper level and in a new way, and I think you will, too. Expect to find simple pleasure, quiet beauty, good humor, and authentic friendship as you spend time with Wil and meet the abbot and his monks one at a time. Wil's account is filled with the small kindnesses, given and received, that we so often take for granted. What we need is what he offers: an invitation to discover a 'spirituality of the ordinary' that leads to a 'stability of heart' that holds us steady in God's love through every circumstance of life."

– **Lisa Myers,** *codirector, CenterQuest School of Spiritual Direction (CQ SSD)*

"Wil invites the reader to share his experience of living within a cloister with these monks who welcomed him 'as Christ,' characteristic of Benedictine and of Filipino hospitality. The daily round of monastic prayer and the rhythms of communal living, with their sacred and mundane character, were catalysts to a deep personal homecoming, to all that is beautiful and uplifting, as well as confronting the broken and flawed parts of himself. The warm fraternity of the monks provided the setting for his reflections, inspirations, and revelations as a person who considers himself still 'under construction.'"

– **Fr. Francis Benedict, OSB,** *Saint Andrew's Abbey, Valyermo, California*

"How does an active oblate learn Benedictine 'stability' when one's eyes tend to follow every thing of beauty that draws their attention? How does one learn Benedictine surrender and obedience when one's heart is filled with many good desires that move him to every direction? ... No matter the litany of 'I should have beens' that Wil admits to in the end, his narrative still clearly points to one thing: God who held him lovingly in God's hands (as did the monks!) while he was stranded and brought him home to real contemplation of 'God in the ordinary' despite distractions arising from the pandemic.... Every reader of Wil's story will surely be nourished and edified reading this piece."

– **Victor R. Baltazar, SJ,** *Jesuit formator, Ignatian Spirituality and Formation Office, Ateneo de Davao University, Philippines*

"Spiritually engaging and delightful! Wil's diary provides glimpses of a 'spirituality on the road' or a spirituality of contemporary life providentially enriched by encountering Benedictine monasticism. Brimming with authenticity, earthiness, and with drizzles of memorable insights from spiritual writers, you will be drawn to Wil's ecumenical spiritual journey captured in heartwarming chronicles of his seemingly forced yet providential time at the abbey."

– **Tim Gener, PhD,** *chancellor and professor of theology, Asian Theological Seminary, Manila, Philippines*

"*Accidental Monk* embodies the magnificence of the Abbey of the Transfiguration with its skies above, which the author describes as 'magically enchanting.' Congratulations to Wil Hernandez, for a scintillating portrayal of the abbey and its monks. In his eloquence with words, Wil speaks of the spirituality and unparalleled hospitality of the Benedictine monks—their patience, obedience, dedication, and even their vulnerabilities. The highlight of the book for me is its chief message of surrender—our ultimate decision to fully trust God no matter what. It not only provides an insight but more so an impetus for one's surrender to God."

– **Gigi Prats,** *president, St. Scholastica's Alumnae Foundation and oblate, Manila Priory of the Missionary Benedictine Sisters of Tutzing*

"Important... it talks about one of the most difficult things to do during this time—to be present, to notice, to see, to feel, to be at home with the ordinary. Thank you, Wil, for sharing with us your experiences of the mundane and the holy ... and for your profound reflections emerging from them."

– **Federico G. Villanueva, PhD,** *author, It's OK to be Not OK: Preaching the Lament Psalms*

"With a good dose of humor, Wil, whom we know as an excellent author and retreat leader, describes his immersion into the life of the contemplative Benedictine community in the Philippines. … An impressive and insightful testimony to how the singing of the Psalms, the attentive and conscious celebration of the Liturgy, and other values of St. Benedict's Rule like silence and hospitality order us and ground us. This unplanned experience helped Wil and can help us to be attentive anew to the amazing beauty of God's creation as well as to God's providential working in our lives even in the midst of a pandemic."

– **Fr. Thomas Leitner, OSB,** *administrator of St. Benedict Center, Schuyler, Nebraska*

"An inspiring narrative. . . . From the initial chaos of cancelled flights and schedules due to COVID-19 pandemic lockdowns, Wil was introduced to a different rhythm of monastic order as he continued to communicate with friends outside the monastery through social media. His prolonged encounter with monastic community life opened a decisive direction on his understanding of spirituality of everyday life that was marked by day-to-day creativity, conversion, and contemplation."

– **Jose V. C. Quilongquilong, SJ,** *former president, Loyola School of Theology, Quezon City, Philippines*

"God seemed to have good-humoredly invited me along an amusing albeit profound journey with Wil, the 'accidental monk.' Many of us will resonate with his struggles with ordinary, common, everyday matters . . . his personal realizations along with his spiritual evolution amidst his grace-filled strandedness—even if our own experience comes from a different situation as we find ourselves ushered by this pilgrim who continues in his surrender to God."

– **Cynch Concepcion-Baga,** *social psychologist, human formation specialist, spiritual companion*

≈≈≈

Accidental Monk

A Chronicle of
Struggle, Faith, and Surrender

WIL HERNANDEZ, PhD, Obl. OSB

CQ RESOURCES
www.CQCenterQuest.org

CenterQuest (CQ) is an ecumenical hub for the study and practice of
Christian spirituality which hosts an international hybrid School
of Spiritual Direction (SSD) program.

Published by:

122A E. Foothill Blvd., PMB 306
Arcadia, CA 91006-2505
1-833-QUEST-05
www.CQCenterQuest.org

To the three
key communities worldwide
of which I am actively a part:

CenterQuest
Henri Nouwen Society
Benedictine Oblates

2021 February

To Julie,

Stay present
& be blessed!

All the best,

Wil

contents

xi   *foreword*

xiii   *preface*

1   *prologue*

9   *Struggle*
March 17 - 31

65   *Faith*
April 1 - 30

163   *Surrender*
May 1 - 26

261   *epilogue*

267   *postface*

273   *afterword*

277   *gratitude*

279   *notes*

foreword

A pandemic can bring on unexpected events. For example, I never expected Bro. Wil Hernandez to write a book about our abbey and its monks. His main purpose in coming here during Holy Week of 2020 was to give a series of talks based on the Holy Rule of St. Benedict, primarily to our monks and oblates. However, Bro. Wil found himself staying in our abbey for more than two months, thus getting to know not only the monks more personally but also what the monastic life is really all about. Never before have we had a guest stay that long inside the enclosure of our abbey, faithfully submitting himself to our set monastic schedule.

As a result of this unplanned immersion experience, Bro. Wil came to be exposed at a deeper level to the dynamics of monastic life and the intricacies of communal living. Contrary to what outsiders usually imagine about monks in general, he witnessed firsthand real human beings, grounded in their humanity and not necessarily living an angelic existence. Daily he found an outlet on Facebook to post and process his thoughts, as well as the insights gleaned during his protracted stay in the abbey.

In a monastery, monks come from very different backgrounds. And these differences become more pronounced as they live together. For to live in close contact with one another requires much patience, tolerance, and forgiveness. Human nature is a mystery. The internal warfare is constant. St. Benedict compares the monastery to a battlefield where one is constantly at war with things not of God and struggling against the tendencies of our human nature.

What Bro. Wil shares with us in his diary (which he patiently reconstructed from his Facebook posts, and in regular consultation with me and the monks, as soon as he returned to Los Angeles) are his personal experiences of monastic living at close range. Having been included as part of the community, he came to be acquainted with the varied personalities of the monks. In more ways than one, Bro. Wil lived and engaged with our community not as a guest but almost as a monk himself—very much like one of us.

One will surely be enriched by Bro. Wil's thoughtful insights, which he now offers as a gift to the outside world after having had the privilege of gaining an intimate look at monastic living. Regardless of whether we are inside or outside a monastery, I think the outstanding reality remains that all of us, in our heart of hearts, desire to live a life of holiness and strive to become closer to Christ.

This is the first time anyone has ever written about monastic life within the context of our Abbey of the Transfiguration. Bro. Wil highlights in these pages an incarnational spirituality that is simultaneously an everyday spirituality that extends out into the world. Wil has richly blessed our community through his time with us, and now, through this chronicle of his experiences, he is ready to bless the wider world, too. I am pleased to recommend Bro. Wil's diary as a most worthy read!

 **Abbot Eduardo Africa, OSB**
Abbey of the Transfiguration
Malaybalay, Bukidnon
Philippines

preface

I never set out to write a diary. The thought wasn't even on my radar. I am not an avid journaler by nature, and I imagined that my scheduled visit to the Abbey of the Transfiguration in April 2020 would be an ordinary stay. After all, this would be my fourth time there, and the third consecutive visit falling on Holy Week, through Easter Monday. What I did not expect, however, was that my visit would be extended, not once or twice but five times, eventually lasting for two months and ten days. "What's the big deal?" you might ask. None really, except that I was completely unprepared for the longer stay. I usually plan my trips abroad a year in advance, with a well-laid-out itinerary. This stop at the abbey was meant to be the final leg of a trip to Asia that began the third week of January and should have ended by mid-April, when I would return to my home and family in Los Angeles.

Interestingly, although I never journaled about my day-to-day experiences in the abbey while I was there, I never missed a day posting something on Facebook, whether it was a photo I had taken, a quote that resonated with me as I scrolled down my news feed, or my sentiment for the day. In this sense, you could say I unintentionally kept a Facebook "journal," with remarkable consistency. So when I finally gave some serious consideration to my friends' insistence that I document my abbey experience in writing, I knew I could count on Facebook to help me reconstruct everything. But I had my share of misgivings about doing so.

To begin with, I balked because I wasn't convinced that my story was sufficiently compelling to merit publishing as a diary. But once I had the luxury to sit down and inventory all that had transpired during the period of my "overstay" at the abbey, I was amazed at the richness of it all. The more I reminisced about my adventures, as well as some misadventures, the more motivated I became to pursue the project, as my initial apprehensions gradually faded away.

Part of my objective during my Asian trip was to insert some focused writing time into my schedule, since I was in the process of finishing a book I had been working on for some time. I was able to do some of that, but much of that project remains unfinished. Thus the notion of adding a new writing project to my already crowded agenda gave me pause. Yet I couldn't shake the idea. Not to go forward with it felt like poor stewardship of what God had entrusted to me. In my heart of hearts, I had a genuine urge to put my experience formally in writing—as tedious as I envisioned the process to be—if only to testify to God's providence, faithfulness, and generous provision throughout my stay at the abbey. Likewise, I could not afford to take for granted God's deep, interior working in my heart through the process, which I don't believe I would have profited from were it not for the many challenging circumstances into which I'd been immersed.

✣ ✣ ✣

Back to my initial hesitations: In all honesty, I also worried my work would be cast as a cheap imitation of Henri Nouwen's hugely popular *The Genesee Diary: Report from a Trappist Monastery,* a book he published in 1981 detailing his seven-month monastic sojourn at the Abbey of the Genesee in upstate New York. And who am I compared to the stature of Nouwen (who is my self-proclaimed patron saint) to dare write something in a similar genre? However, upon further deliberation, I realized that there were notable differences in our respective contexts. For one, Nouwen's entry into the Abbey of the Genesee was deliberate and planned; mine was totally unplanned. He was an ordained priest who requested to become a temporary monk for a specified period of time; I am a Benedictine oblate (a lay associate connected to a local monastery) who accidentally became immersed in the monastic life out of sheer providence, for an undetermined season. The one commonality is that both our experiences transpired in a Benedictine monastery.

Moreover, our main sources and delivery methods are somewhat distinct. While Nouwen's accounts can readily be classified as classic diary entries, mine are compiled from a variety of media, beginning with my own Facebook posts and including photographs I took on my iPhone, visual graphics containing quotations (my own and others'), and featured news articles and video clips, as well as some choice poetry. All of these reflect the social media world in which I naturally revolve, so in one sense it's not an extraordinary collection. But if I were to lay claim to something truly unique about my experience, it would be that it did not take place under what would be considered normal circumstances, as Nouwen's did. My unexpected immersion into monasticism came about against the backdrop of an escalating global pandemic and all the attendant uncertainties.

In this book I intend primarily to chronicle my own monastery experience in the midst of the COVID-19 lockdown. On the whole, it serves to highlight my monastic immersion as an oblate, consequently heightening my already growing appreciation for Benedictine spirituality. In certain ways, it is the unfolding narrative of my personal struggles and triumphs under the massive "cloud of unknowing" brought on by the repercussions of the ongoing pandemic.

I also hope that this book will provide you with a glimpse into a monastic community populated by goodhearted but perfectly imperfect people, whom I had the privilege of knowing—up close and personal. On one hand, I was transported into another world, one I had long presumed to be familiar territory only to have my own considerable ignorance exposed. On the other hand, I learned that even though the world these monks inhabit is markedly different from my own, at the end of the day, we're all clothed with the same raw humanity. If there is one thing for which I am grateful in light of the privileged exposure I had, it is the demystification of my own limited understanding of the monastic life, now stripped of its many distortions and idealizations that have unwittingly clouded my perceptions over the years.

In these accounts, I speak as a lay Benedictine oblate of Saint Andrew's Abbey in Valyermo, California, where I stayed for nearly six months in early 2004 while completing my doctoral dissertation on Henri Nouwen. As an oblate, I consider myself a lifelong student of the Rule of St. Benedict, and over the years I have conducted many retreats in Benedictine venues all over the United States and beyond. In 2019, I was privileged to join a Benedictine pilgrimage in Germany, Austria, and Switzerland, hosted by St. Benedict Center in Schuyler, Nebraska, where I also regularly conduct Nouwen retreats. Through my PhD concentration on Christian spirituality, I gained a basic familiarity with monastic history and tradition and have maintained a keen and ever-growing interest in it.

A month prior to landing at the Abbey of the Transfiguration on this recent trip to the Philippines, I had the opportunity to conduct a weekend retreat in a Carmelite-run spirituality center close to Bacolod City (Negros Occidental), on the topic of everyday spirituality based on the Benedictine core values of stability, obedience, and conversion applied in daily life. Since I had been concentrating much of my energy on this broad topic for more than a year prior to my Asian trip, I thought it best to focus on the same topic for the series of talks I was scheduled to deliver at the Abbey of the Transfiguration during Holy Week. This was a deliberate attempt to be more strategic in my investment of time, energy, and effort to coincide with my current passion for making Benedictine spirituality relevant to ordinary folks living ordinary lives. In fact, after finishing my monthlong teaching stint at Loyola School of Theology in Metro Manila toward the end of February, I sat down with the dean and proposed the same theme for my spirituality course offering next year, to which he readily agreed.

In the interest of full disclosure, I also want to make clear that I write as an Episcopalian by affiliation, although I take a highly ecumenical stance—that is, I openly embrace all faith traditions and denominations within the Christian mainstream and express this concretely in all of my ministry work. Based on the influence of Henri Nouwen, whose enduring spiritual legacy I have committed to propagating, mine is an ecumenical spirit and practice largely patterned after his.

Like most Filipinos, I grew up Catholic—a devout one at that (as a kid I even dreamed of becoming a priest). I left my faith tradition as a freshman in college to become a Baptist—moving from Fundamental to Conservative to Southern to American Baptist over the years. I previously worked with an international, interdenominational parachurch organization for eighteen years and completed a master's degree in theology at an evangelical Protestant seminary and a doctorate at an evangelical-ecumenical seminary, with additional studies at two Catholic universities in the United States, concentrating in spirituality.

Some twelve years ago I settled into being an Episcopalian because I still found myself subscribing to Protestant theology, at least its major strands, while reembracing many aspects of Catholic sacramentality and liturgy. In a way, I have come to love and embrace the best of both worlds. Becoming an Episcopalian was the closest I could get to "coming home." Truth be told, there was even a period when I seriously considered becoming an Episcopal priest.

After becoming an oblate of a Catholic Benedictine monastery a decade ago, as well as teaching and leading retreats in predominantly Catholic settings for more than fifteen years while maintaining my ecumenical thrust, I have tended to lean heavily into my Catholic roots, relearning and reappreciating my tradition of origin. I am keenly aware, without a doubt, that Catholic blood continues to flow through my veins.

I share all of this backstory to drive home a point. In entering into the monastery setting at the abbey, I was conscious that I did so without starting from a blank slate. I came with certain perceived advantages, which I thought at first would enable me to fit in more easily: my good Catholic upbringing, my advanced Catholic education and training in spirituality (including spiritual formation and spiritual direction, and basic exposure to monastic studies and literature), my Nouwen connections (as a teacher and retreat leader), and most importantly my Benedictine affiliation as an oblate.

However, I was also cognizant that I carried some baggage, for better or worse: my strong ecumenical sentiments and my Episcopalian via media ("middle way") ethos—an amalgam of both Protestant and Catholic expressions and sensitivities. And I had come to this juncture in my journey bearing a rising burden directly related to my Christian identity. For the past six years I have been earnestly wrestling with issues of both identity and belongingness.

At bottom for me lies the elementary question of whether, by heart conviction, I identify (and thus belong) as a Catholic or as a Protestant. In my ecumenical positioning and my Episcopalian affiliation, I've known what it's like to straddle both worlds, which I've been equally comfortable to inhabit. For a long time, I thought this should put the issue to rest for me and that I could live with this next-to-ideal arrangement (or compromise).

Yet when I returned to the Abbey of the Transfiguration in 2020, I could no longer deny my heart's longing to settle into my truest home, whichever it might be and whatever it might take. At the same time, apprehensions, questions, and concerns continued to plague me, impressing upon me that a firm resolution to my lingering struggle might not yet be at hand. All of these thoughts were present to me as I entered into the monastic territory with which I presumed to be relatively familiar.

What I didn't realize was that all of my studies and exposure to all things Benedictine would become practically insignificant compared to my actual experience of "overstaying" at the abbey, where I was plunged into the living reality of monastic life. There I was able to experience firsthand what I had only theorized or philosophized about before. For one thing, I didn't strictly fall into the category of a normal guest in the monastery; I was allowed to stay inside the enclosure.

Soon enough, I started participating actively in the liturgies and other monastic activities on a regular basis, so much so that I found myself following and eventually flowing into the community's established rhythms. I want to emphasize that I was the only non-monk living with the monks, so you could say I was stuck with them and they were stuck with me! I guess I became an "accidental" monk!

Two months and ten days may seem brief to some, but during that period of time the monastery became my world—the world I woke up to and went to sleep to every single day. I'd be lying if I didn't admit to relishing the initial romanticized phase of my stay, but that soon wore off as I became aware that this would be my new reality—and who knew for how long?—so I had better accept it. For a while I wrestled with my newfound "normal." It's not an exaggeration to say that those two months seemed like forever to me, accustomed as I was to a way of life in the United States where I was pretty much in command. At the abbey I had to learn to release my need for control, ever so slowly and never without at least a tinge of struggle.

Despite my wavering reluctance, my experience there afforded me many critical opportunities to deeply reflect upon my ever-evolving understanding and application of what everyday spirituality is truly about. In turn, this naturally influenced how I learned to live out the concrete realities of my professed theology and my practical ministry within the vital context of community.

✢ ✢ ✢

Far from landing in a kind of prison in the abbey, I was quite fortunate to have been stranded in a paradise of sorts. But I did have the sense of wandering, of being lost in this "paradise," time and again. Still, I could not be more than thankful that I had ended up there during the lockdown, and I could not have pictured myself being stuck anywhere else, especially not Metro Manila! In more ways than one, this was for me a welcome exile. There was absolutely no reason to complain, but I still managed to find some at times—much to my shame!

Who would not be enthralled by the rich natural beauty of the monastery's setting? Nestled on a hill in the village of Malaybalay—the capital city of the province of Bukidnon, which is situated in the northern region of Mindanao—the Abbey of the Transfiguration was inaugurated as a monastery in 1983 and subsequently elevated to the official status of abbey in 2017, with the Rt. Rev. Abbot Eduardo Africa, OSB as its first abbot. The pyramidal structure of the chapel—designed by no less than the National Artist for Architecture, the late Leandro Locsin—figures as its most prominent landmark.

The abbey's name was inspired by the recorded account found in the synoptic Gospels (Mt 17:1–8, Mk 9:2–8, Lk 9:28–36), where Peter broaches the idea to Jesus of building three tents for him and the two prophets, Moses and Elijah. Thus in the original structure of the monastery (now referred to as the "old monastery"), not too far from where the present church is located, three pyramid-motif tents were constructed, reminiscent of the familiar Transfiguration scene. It is worth noting that the first survey visit to the site, on August 6, 1981, fell on the Feast of the Transfiguration. The visit was headed by Abbot Ed—Fr. Ed then—along with the Most Rev. Francisco Claver, SJ, then the bishop of Malaybalay, who had offered the land. They unanimously decided that this would be the most suitable place for their monastic foundation, a decision that was unmistakably led by God.

According to Abbot Ed, during the monastery's early days, the locals, who were mostly unfamiliar with the concept of the Transfiguration, found the abbey's name not only strange sounding but also difficult to pronounce. A few referred to it as the Monastery of the Configuration, and one person sent him a letter hilariously addressed to the Monastery of Transportation. All that has changed. Over the years, the abbey has become widely known and even regarded as a tourist destination in Mindanao, to the point that the local government has even shouldered the expenses for the paved road leading up to the abbey.

Little did I know that this hidden paradise would serve as God's appointed home for me for more than two months, as a series of lockdowns was imposed throughout the Philippines and the world. It was to be the longest two and a half months of my life until then, and destined to be a significant interlude in my fast-paced existence. In the company of twelve Benedictine monks, my life took a radical turn within what I now see as a relatively brief period of time. This short season of divine interruption is what I aim to chronicle here.

～～～

The Abbey Church with its pyramid motif

prologue

January 22, 2020: the day I was to fly out of Los Angeles to the Philippines. A friend from Manila texted me to advise that I should wear a face mask, since I'd be on a direct flight for fourteen hours nonstop. At first I didn't think the COVID-19 infection was all that serious, but it seemed sensible enough to travel with adequate protection, just in case. So with less than half an hour before my Lyft pick-up to go to the airport, my wife, Juliet, started calling different stores to check on their stock of masks. Much to our surprise, the nearby CVS, Target, and Walgreens were sold out. I ended up running to a Home Depot store about ten minutes away, only to be left without much choice but to take what was available on their shelf: N-95 masks—the kind professional painters wear on their jobs.

At the Tom Bradley International terminal at Los Angeles International Airport, it became obvious to me that mask-wearing was to be expected. With the type of mask I had, it was difficult to breathe comfortably, but I made it through the entire plane ride without removing my gear except when eating. When I arrived at the Manila airport, the scene looked somewhat different: evidently mask-wearing there was optional, so I felt more relaxed. The scenario changed again when I went back to the airport two days later for my trip to Taiwan to conduct a community retreat for the International Teresian sisters. This time I observed a lot more people wearing face masks all over the airport. And in Taipei, those not wearing masks definitely stood out. The message was loud and clear: mask was a must. Because I was stationed for most of the week inside a retreat center in Hualien, about three hours from Taipei, I didn't have a good sense of what was going on, as far as COVID-19 was concerned. It wasn't until I flew back to Manila on February 2 that I realized I could've been stuck in Taiwan had I delayed my flight by one day, which had been my original intent. I was glad that I had decided to leave earlier so I could devote a day to unpacking and repacking for my next leg of teaching commitments: a four-week course on the spirituality of Henri Nouwen at the Loyola School of Theology in Quezon City (Metro Manila).

When I checked in the following day at the Loyola House of Studies, I was immediately alerted that two of my Jesuit students had gotten stranded in Taiwan; they were allowed to travel back to Manila later that week, after making an appeal to the Philippine Embassy. Now it was starting to dawn on me that this COVID-19 phenomenon must really be something to reckon with. Yet for the duration of my stay at the Jesuit house, hardly anybody wore masks. I did not wear one while in the classroom and during mealtimes, and neither did most everybody with whom I spent time there. In between teaching, I even managed to fly to another island in the Visayas to conduct a weekend retreat, and overall things appeared quite normal. It seemed there was nothing to be concerned about.

After a month of teaching, I checked out of the Loyola campus on February 27 and spent two nights at the Abbey of Our Lady of Montserrat, just inside the campus of San Beda University, which is run by Benedictine monks. I was there for an afternoon of meetings with selected folks involved in our CenterQuest-Asia endeavor. CenterQuest (CQ) is the ecumenical organization I co-founded in early 2013, which hosts an international School of Spiritual Direction (SSD) program. For the past several years I've been making trips to Southeast Asia in hopes of eventually establishing a CQ extension in Manila for Asian countries.

At the abbey in Manila, I wasn't aware that the local situation with COVID-19 was gradually worsening, despite warnings I had received from worried friends urging me to cancel my ten-day trip to Singapore, which was scheduled to begin in two days. In fact, the night before my departure, my housemates and I even went out for dinner at Bonifacio Global City (BGC)—an impressively high-end hangout comparable to, if not more spectacular than, the ones we have in Los Angeles. (I was staying with a group of men involved with Companions of the Redeemer, based in a village in Parañaque close to the airport.) Shortly thereafter, we proceeded to the nearby theater to watch a reimagined contemporary version of the *Joseph the Dreamer* musical staged by Trumpets, a local theater outfit managed by a number of my artist friends in Metro Manila, with whom I had the chance to reconnect briefly before and after the show. It was an instant reunion with old friends in the local entertainment industry. (Back in the '90s, I used to direct a ministry to music and movie entertainers called Artists-in-Touch.) The whole atmosphere of the evening was charged with excitement—jubilant and carefree—with no premonition of any impending shift in mood.

I pushed through with my travel to Singapore the following morning after some assurance from people I trusted that I would not be quarantined when I got back to Manila. However, I proceeded with caution, well aware that Singapore was under strict COVID-19 monitoring. Knowing beforehand that, for the most part, I would be holed up inside Montfort Retreat Centre without any other guests around, I willingly took the calculated risk. My encounters with people took place mainly at the retreat center, and I only went out a few times, and never to crowded places. A Filipino priest-friend of mine, Fr. RV, who is temporarily stationed in a parish in Singapore, brought me one day to the prominent ION Orchard, which to me resembled a ghost town compared to the overcrowded mall scene I was accustomed to seeing in Metro Manila.

In retrospect, my Singapore stint was well worth the risk, since the trip proved to be very productive and strategic as far as our

CenterQuest-Asia networking effort was concerned. Still, I felt a bit anxious returning to Manila, for fear that I'd be detained for quarantine. But my brief time at the airport turned out to be hassle-free. This increased my confidence as I projected the subsequent trips I had lined up to Mindanao, a southern island of the Philippines. I only had one night to attend to my usual unpacking-repacking drill. My frequent traveling has taught me well to travel light, and I had to be quite deliberate in what I packed and left behind—just enough to get me by during my monthlong, three-city trip to Butuan City, Surigao City, and Malaybalay, Bukidnon, home to the Abbey of the Transfiguration, where I was to spend my Holy Week until Easter Monday.

Little did I know that with my exit from Manila on March 12, all of my well-laid plans were about to be altered. That same evening, the president of the Philippines announced a major lockdown for Metro Manila. If I had left a day later, I probably wouldn't have made it to Butuan because of travel bans (including both inbound and outbound flights at the Manila airport), and I would've left more than forty registered retreatants in Butuan hanging. At first I feared that the retreat itself would be cancelled, but since it was mostly for the Missionary Sisters of Mary, with just a few outsiders participating, the event proceeded as planned. After a very fruitful weekend spent there at the San Lorenzo Ruiz Pastoral Center, a ban on mass gatherings was imposed throughout the city. Fortunately we were given a special dispensation to celebrate Mass that Sunday as a concluding event for our small crowd inside the center.

Rumors swirled of impending lockdowns in nearby cities, such as Cagayan de Oro, where COVID-19 cases seemed to be escalating at an alarming rate. Sr. Maribel, a Benedictine nun and my point person for the string of trips within Mindanao, determined it was best not to proceed to Surigao City for our planned public symposium at the Bishop's Residence. Admittedly, I felt disappointed because I was so looking forward to visiting Surigao for the first time. I had also scheduled some focused writing time there. Sr. Maribel—or Sr. M, my term of endearment for her—happened to be a current participant in our CenterQuest School of Spiritual Direction program, and I really wanted to see the monastery that she had founded. But I understood the wisdom in the decision, so we agreed it would be safer for me to proceed directly to the abbey in Malaybalay, on Thursday. This was three weeks earlier than my planned Holy Week stay.

There I was on Tuesday, thinking that I would savor a little downtime after the recent retreat, when Sr. M rang me up to inform me that Malaybalay would be on lockdown, too. Therefore we should plan on leaving in two hours, before we got stuck somewhere. Though mentally unprepared, I conceded, so off we headed after lunch toward Bukidnon—approximately an eight-hour drive from Butuan depending on who's driving!

Joined by Sr. M's coworker, Sr. Virgie, in the SUV, the three of us embarked on a speedy three-and-a-half-hour drive to Gaisano Puerto Mall in Cagayan de Oro. (Sr. M, I discovered, is quite a driver!) There, I was to be picked up by a van arranged by the abbey. The whole drive threw me into a dizzy spell. For one, I hadn't slept enough the night before and was dead tired; for another, we traveled through winding roads during the rain, and I suffer from motion sickness; and finally, Sr. M was apparently on her typical fast track! As a nun, she might be engaged with all things contemplative, but slow driving was definitely not one of those things. During the drive, when I couldn't stand it anymore, I rolled down my window to catch some fresh air. In cases like this, I recalled the ever-reliable "White Flower" oil that my wife insists I carry with me at all times. Smelling the menthol aroma of this eucalyptus oil never fails to ward off my dizzy spells, except this time I didn't have any with me. But Sr. M, ever prepared, came to my rescue as she pulled from one of the secret pockets of her habit a perfect equivalent: efficascent oil, which helped revive me fairly quickly.

As expected, Loury, the monastery-hired driver (famous for his skilled maneuverings), was already there waiting for us in the parking lot at the Gaisano Puerto Mall. It was long past 5 P.M. and I felt mildly hungry. After a quick break, we bid goodbye to Sr. M and Sr. Virgie and I went with Loury, who briefed me that it would normally take close to two hours to reach the abbey. On that note, I didn't feel the urgency to grab a bite before we took off, which proved to be a big mistake, as I discovered later.

Soon after we left, we found ourselves stuck in a very long line of vehicles, mostly huge transport trucks. For the next hour or so, as it was slowly getting dark, we hardly moved. Initially I didn't mind our snail's pace; my body was too exhausted to react, so I just slept for almost an hour, only to wake up to find we were going at exactly the same pace. Then I started to get restless, not to mention hungry. It became clear to me that this was going to be a much longer trip than I had prepared for. During heavy traffic in the Philippines, it is normal for two lanes to turn into three, and Loury wisely shifted into the third one as soon as he could. (And thank God he did; otherwise we could've been stranded in that traffic forever.) Embarrassing as it is for me to reveal, I had to disembark three times from the van to slip over to the dark side of the road to empty my bladder. It is a normal occurrence in the Philippines, but I was no longer used to witnessing this, let alone doing it myself. After the second time around, I frankly couldn't care less; I just wanted to reach our destination in one piece.

Finally, after four and a half hours that seemed like eternity, we arrived at the checkpoint between Misamis Oriental and Bukidnon. We were required to take a foot bath and have our temperatures taken—a mere three-minute check considering all those hours of traffic we'd been subjected to! The hour after that was practically traffic-free. Loury quickly got back into his element and sped through the winding road leading up to Malaybalay. Under ordinary circumstances, I would've held on for dear life while Loury drove at such high speed, but truthfully I was grateful he went so fast. All I could think of was getting to the abbey and crashing into bed straightaway—actually, eating first because I was so famished I would gobble up anything the monastery would feed me.

At almost 11 P.M., Dom Carlo, the abbey guest master was still wide awake and ready to greet us as we alighted from the van. After a quick meal, he ushered me into the monastery enclosure and straight to the guest room at the very end of the cloister. Although I was totally exhausted, the first thing I did was check the internet signal in my room. To my delight, it worked without a hitch (and my laptop even remembered the network password from last year's visit). Breathing a deep sigh of relief as I lay in bed, I reflected on what had just transpired, still totally unsuspecting of the adventure awaiting me in the next couple of months at the abbey.

Thus my chronicle begins . . .

〜〜〜

Struggle

March 17-31

"To struggle is to begin
to see the world differently."

− JOAN CHITTISTER

17 MARCH
tuesday

The Morning After

I woke up late on my first morning at the abbey. Consequently I missed the 5 A.M. Lauds (Morning Prayer), which I meant to attend so I could make my dramatic appearance before all the monks gathered at the main chapel. Well, so much for that plan. On top of getting up late, I could feel my head mildly spinning.

Worse, I was a bit annoyed to find out that the internet signal, which registered quite strongly just last night, seemed to have stopped working. I recalled from my previous year's visit how moody the signal could sometimes be on this wing of the monastery. Because I primarily do my work with our CenterQuest School of Spiritual Direction online, good internet connectivity is a big deal for me—my lifework orbits around it.

The first person who came to mind was Dom Pietro, the "techie" monk at the abbey. How could I possibly forget him? Dom Pietro had always set up the mic and the slide projector for the retreat presentations I've done for the past three years at the abbey. He has perfected the drill and was prepared to come to my rescue always—well, almost always.

Two years ago, we were all gathered at 9 A.M. at the Abbey Museum with no Dom Pietro in sight—and no sound system and projector set up. Nobody knew where he was. That's not entirely true. Dom Pietro has the tendency to oversleep and the monks know that well. As they had predicted, he was in his room, deep asleep. Other than that, he's a pretty reliable guy!

And who did I run into this morning in the corridor on my way to the Abbey Guest House for breakfast? Dom Pietro, thank God! I blurted out my complaint, bracing myself for his standard response: "It's always like that here." But to my surprise, Dom Pietro had a ready solution for my pressing need to get connected on Zoom that morning. He dissolved my worries in an instant. He directed me to one of the small conference rooms in the Abbey Administration Building, where the internet connection was guaranteed to work all the time—except when there was a brownout (which, I would learn later, occurred more frequently than usual during summertime). I dashed into the room and happily set up my laptop on the long wooden table.

From that point on, that same conference room became my permanent office—until I found out I'd soon have a competitor for the internet signal in the adjacent room, no less than the abbot himself, who could not stand the sometimes painfully slow, "contemplative" signal in his own room. Now I gained an office neighbor in Abbot Ed, whom I enjoyed disturbing every now and then and who learned over time to graciously put up with my occasional intrusions, sometimes in the middle of his Facebook time.

✦ ✦ ✦

Right before midday prayer, the abbot stopped me as I was passing through the sacristy on my way to the chapel, and the first thing that came out of his mouth made my day. He noted how I seemed to have lost weight since the last time I was there and that I looked good. Secretly I congratulated myself that my forty-day Lenten fast from sugar was apparently working to my advantage—even if it was mainly for vanity's sake.

After prayer, I was pleased that Abbot Ed decided to join me for lunch at the guest house, where I freely unloaded on him the blow-by-blow account of our travel ordeal last night. We had a fruitful time catching up with each other. In the course of our conversation, Abbot Ed gave me a heads-up about the Lenten Recollection scheduled during Holy Week, when I was supposed to do a series of talks on the topic of everyday spirituality (drawing from the Rule of St. Benedict).

Although I had qualms about it, because of the social distancing measures we were required to follow, he nevertheless expressed his optimism about pushing through with the plan, with some modifications. (Abbot Ed is an eternal optimist, I've discovered!) He wanted to limit the attendees exclusively to his monks, instead of the general public who normally would flock to the abbey throughout Holy Week. This generated some anxiety in me. My entire audience would be the resident monks, whom I assumed knew the Rule backward and forward. I did not relish the idea of "preaching to the choir." I attempted to persuade the abbot to drop the plan under the pretext that we should abide by the government prohibition against group gatherings. To my brilliant proposition he simply responded with a measured sense of tentativeness, and we agreed to "wait and see" (although in my mind I remained quite determined to win him over to forgetting the whole thing).

✣ ✣ ✣

I ended my day feeling like I'd missed something. To my utter regret, I realized that I'd completely forgotten the birthday of my oldest brother, Rolly, who lives in my hometown of Calamba, Laguna (the birthplace of our national hero, José Rizal, who happened to be our "neighbor," since his famous national shrine is just a stone's throw away from where my family lived). I felt awful for having failed to greet my *kuya* (older brother), even via Facebook—something I've never done before. Boy, I must've been so disoriented to have overlooked the date.

Later it dawned on me that it was also St. Patrick's Day—a widely observed celebration in the United States—which has always prompted me to remember my kuya's birthday ever since I migrated to the US some twenty-five years ago. I don't recall hearing any mention of St. Patrick here in the abbey—a reminder that I'm not in America—and I'm a bit curious as to why.

18 MARCH
wednesday

My Newfound Home

After Lauds, I hurriedly took my breakfast at the guest house and primed myself in my newfound office to do spiritual direction via Zoom with a longtime directee residing in Guatemala City. Rarely have I initiated a time of focused prayer at the end of our sessions, but I felt strongly moved to do so today, in light of the worldwide pandemic we are all facing. While deep in prayer I felt overcome by the reality that I was so far away from my own family in Los Angeles, and it led to feeling very apprehensive and overwhelmed by many other things—real and imagined—that were starting to play out wildly in my mind.

The comforting promise of Philippians 4:6–7 suddenly became so palpable to me after hearing my directee invoke a portion of it during our prayer. It grabbed hold of my anxious heart and began flooding me with a sense of peace I had not experienced in a very long while.

Do not worry about anything,
but in everything by prayer and supplication

with thanksgiving let your requests
be made known to God.
And the peace of God, which surpasses
all understanding, will guard your hearts
and your minds in Christ Jesus.

I very seldom post passages of scripture on my Facebook timeline, especially such a familiar, oft-quoted one. On this particular occasion, however, I felt the urge to do just that, and I boldly invited all of my Facebook friends to focus on this verse and claim it for themselves just as I did this morning. It was my way of passing on the peace to others, I guess.

✢ ✢ ✢

Scanning the view outside my office window, I sensed for the first time since I arrived the stillness of my surroundings. After a hectic one and a half months of traveling from Manila to Taiwan, Singapore, and various parts of the Philippines, teaching and doing workshops and retreats, here before me was this serene place to which God graciously brought me to settle down—with ample time and space to reflect, ponder, pray, write, and commune with God in silence.

To be with this community in this place at this time is God's lavish gift to me.

In the quiet of my heart I murmured, "This is home for me now, together with my Benedictine family. With their characteristic hospitality, I am warmly welcomed here. To be with this community in this place at this time is God's lavish gift to me. For this I cannot but be grateful!"

19 MARCH
thursday

Aloneness and Loneliness

Today was another characteristically quiet day. I've been accustomed to seeing a lot of people around the abbey during each of my prior visits, especially closer to Holy Week. Now the whole place looks empty—and lonely to me. This is an unfamiliar sight and I'm not used to it. I've only been here a few days and already I am feeling the first stab of both aloneness and loneliness.

Thankfully, this evening after dinner at the guest house with a couple other retreatants, faithfully practicing social distancing, Abbot Ed stopped me on my way back to my room and invited me to join the monks at the Refectory for some dessert. At first I wanted to beg off since I was on my Lenten fast—no sweets—but the abbot reminded me that it was the Feast of St. Joseph. Now that sounded to me like a good enough excuse, so the sweet tooth in me prevailed and I gladly and quickly gave in!

Since this was my first time joining everyone in the dining hall, I was a little shy. Moreover, I felt hesitant entering their territory. Both feelings, however, would quickly subside in the weeks to come, as I felt more at ease encountering the monks on their own turf.

| The Abbey Guest House (above) and Refectory (below)

20 MARCH
friday

A New and Refreshing View

With not much else to do on an idle Friday afternoon, I thought about loitering around the abbey grounds—my way of doing a kind of visual inspection of the place that I've never had the occasion to explore. For my past three visits, my focus has been on my retreat talks, with very little opportunity to simply enjoy the scenery. But with ample time on my hands, now was my chance!

Noticing that the nearby Abbey Gift Shop was open, I settled there for a while. The shop has expanded a bit since the last time I visited, with the Abbey Café added to it. The small café has a nice sitting area with wide glass sliding doors through which one can see the vast field outside, with some cattle grazing lazily. Having been immersed in the concrete jungle of Los Angeles, with hardly any green in sight, this refreshing view was a definite upside to my temporary exile.

I ordered the only instant green tea available and for the next half hour or so I just whiled away my time at the tiny square table, sipping my not-so-hot tea. It dawned on me that I was the only customer at the café savoring the pleasant view. When I emerged, I felt peaceful and lighthearted as I proceeded to the chapel for 5 P.M. Vespers (Evening Prayer).

The cattle field beside the Abbey Gift Shop |

21 MARCH
saturday

Reasons to Celebrate

For Benedictines worldwide, today is a special feast day in honor of the father of Western monasticism, St. Benedict of Nursia. It is one of the two commemorated feasts in his name in the Roman calendar—today being the memorial of his death and July 11 being the memorial of his birth.

I also have a personal reason to celebrate this day. Ten years ago, I first made my vow to live according to the Rule of St. Benedict as a lay oblate of Saint Andrew's Abbey in Valyermo, California. During the early morning Mass officiated by Abbot Ed, I was afforded the chance to renew my vow publicly at the main chapel with a few abbey friends in attendance, among them Mayet (and her husband, Mawi) and Kristin, who even prepared some local *tortas* (like cupcakes) for us to enjoy at the guest house immediately afterward.

For dinner, I was again invited to join the monks at the Refectory for community celebration, which became another welcome occasion to conveniently break my Lenten sugar fast—it was St. Benedict's feast day, after all!

✢ ✢ ✢

As I reflect back on this day, I admit that I had fantasized that this anniversary of renewing my vow as a Benedictine oblate might also be the day to finally put to rest the nagging predicament of my Protestant/Catholic ambivalence, which has been bothering me for so long—that this March 21, here in the abbey in the Philippines, might be my final "coming home" or "coming out" to tell the world of my ultimate decision to fully return to the Catholic fold.

This did not happen for several reasons. For sure, I am distracted by the immediacy of the pandemic and I feel it is too soon to focus on my own issue (although I could be unconsciously downplaying the pressing nature of my dilemma because of my continuing ambivalence about confronting it head on). Also, I have not had the opportunity to discuss any of this with the abbot beforehand, although I so wanted to have some serious conversations with him as I wrestle with this matter.

The bottom line: I am not convinced that I am completely ready. I believe it's best to let go of the idea for the time being and continue to discern God's leading and timing for me. Though there is no resolution in sight, somehow I feel genuine peace in my heart to leave the issue as it is.

22 MARCH
sunday

Claiming My Right to Write

One of the things I aim to accomplish during this extended Asian trip is to deliberately insert some focused writing time into my schedule. Since I ended up coming to the abbey three weeks early because of the lockdowns, I figure perhaps God is granting me some wide-open time and space to attend to my writing here. I am already more than halfway through the draft of the chapters I've been working on for quite some time. Of course, there have been countless interruptions along the way that have made it tougher for me to sustain my momentum. This time I am determined to get back in the saddle and write. As a symbolic act of commencing my writing journey here, I have posted on my Facebook timeline a pledge to myself to reclaim my commitment to the task I've set out to do:

Alright,
I'm right now exercising
my right to write!
Help me, St. Ben!

What better time to start than during my first Sunday in this ideal venue? After breakfast, I went straight to my office and laid several folders containing my rough drafts on the long wooden table, along with some books and other resources I planned to read or review. Looking at all my materials spread out, I was beyond excited!

Just as I was about to kickstart the process, I remembered the soiled clothes that I needed to wash. Knowing the time it would take, I decided to get the wash cycle started before I got engrossed in my writing project, so I rushed back to my room to pick up my clothes and bring them to the laundry room. Dom Carlo was there with laundry detergent to spare and quickly showed me how to program what looked to me like a complicated computerized washer. Confident that it would automatically cycle its way through, I left the washer and returned to the office to refocus on my writing.

As I was thumbing through my manuscript to pick up where I had left off, my attention turned to a book I'd recently ordered from Amazon: *Contemplation and Community: A Gathering of Fresh Voices for a Living Tradition.* I put down my manuscript and picked up the book. At first I was only planning to skim the contents, but I soon found myself reading and underlining major portions of the book for the next two hours. It was a rich read—much too deep to read only once. I was so absorbed that I almost forgot my clothes in the washer, which should've been ready for the dryer by then. I ran back to the laundry room, only to find that the washer had stopped working midway through the unfinished cycle. Since the machine was computerized, I was at a loss for what to do, other than tinker with its different buttons a few times until it started spinning again.

Back at the office, I was unable to resume my interrupted reading. I kept feeling the urge to check my laundry again. So after thirty minutes, I went back. To my utter dismay, the machine had stopped again! Staring blankly at its computerized buttons, I felt like an idiot for not being able to operate a washing machine—even at a monastery in the Philippines! In the US, I always do my own laundry with a click of a button, while here I couldn't get the machine to work for the life of me. Finally I swallowed my pride and sought out Dom Carlo. After I whined about the abbey's complicated high-tech washer, he volunteered to take over from there—bless his heart!

When I returned to the office, I felt my momentum going steadily downhill. As hard as I tried to get back into the writing zone, I simply could not recover from the interruption with the washing machine, so I gave up trying to work. Despite the visual reminder of the Facebook quote I'd posted earlier staring back at me from my computer screen, I knew that my initial drive had tapered off and was beyond recovery. It was time to pack up.

As I was about to close the book I was so fixated on, a familiar name jumped out from the page—Bo Karen Lee, from Princeton Seminary and a colleague of mine from the Society for the Study of Christian Spirituality. For the longest time I had been meaning to get in touch with her about a potential collaboration related to our CenterQuest work. Now, convinced that this unexpected reminder to do so was not mere coincidence but providential, I made sure to note on my to-do list to connect with her ASAP.

Before I knew it, the bell was ringing for midday prayer and I ended the morning feeling that my motivation to write had just evaporated into thin air.

Given my commitment to maximize the opportunity to write while here in the abbey, I promised to redeem myself immediately after lunch by continuing what I had started. Indeed, the spirit was more than willing, but the flesh was becoming weak. I succumbed instead to engaging in the practice of *naptio divina* (divine napping, or siesta) for the better part of the afternoon, until it was almost time for Vespers.

| The Abbey Administration Building where I set up my office

23 MARCH
monday

Discovering Foto Divina

One of my favorite Benedictine authors is Sr. Joan Chittister, a most articulate and prolific writer whose spiritual wisdom never fails to capture my imagination and speak to my soul. Today was no exception. Her weekly e-newsletter *Vision and Viewpoint* delivered this timely message about the essence of commitment:

> **Commitment is the quality of human nature that tells us not to count days or months or years, conversations of efforts or rejections, but simply how to go on going on.**

It was timely not just because I've been mulling over this same subject in relation to the talk I was originally scheduled to give during Holy Week under the Benedictine core value of stability, but also because it was undoubtedly speaking to my present situation.

How exactly do you "go on going on" when you find yourself in the dark? I must confess, I have literally been counting days, especially in light of rumors that the lockdown declared by the Philippine president may extend beyond April 14. Cringing at the possibility of getting stranded in the abbey, it's easy to allow my pregnant imagination to intensify my anxiety.

Not wanting to allow my mind to dwell further on such a thought, I deliberately channeled my energy elsewhere by walking around the monastery to explore areas I have not gone to before—such as the Oratory, whose transparent glass front wall overlooks the majestic mountain outside the enclosure. Psalm 121:1–2 flashed through my mind as I gazed outside while I captured the moment with my iPhone camera.

I lift up my eyes to the hills—from where will my help come? My help comes from the LORD, who made heaven and earth.

From there I continued walking and found myself taking more pictures. It was as though this was the first time I had laid eyes on the mountains encircling the abbey. They're so lush and green, unlike Southern California's brown and barren mountains. Bukidnon is truly beautiful, and the views of the mountains and rolling hills are a visual feast and quite magical to behold.

In this experience I rediscovered my fascination with picture-taking as a way to document in a contemplative way all that I was seeing with intention and conscious effort—*foto divina,* as my friend Renchi from Manila calls it. (This newfound spiritual exercise would yield countless photos during the coming weeks that would prove soul-nourishing for me and sustain me for what lay ahead.)

The sight of the mountains and hills surrounding the abbey

✣ ✣ ✣

At dinner tonight I was joined once more by the abbot in the guest house. As a way of letting the whole world know—yes, via Facebook—that the monastery was "religiously" practicing social distancing, we staged a fun shot of us facing each other from the opposite ends of the very long table. The abbot was a more than willing subject!

| Social distancing staged shot with the Abbot

24 MARCH
tuesday

Divine Synchronicity

S ince I got to the abbey, I have found most morning temperatures fairly cool. Without me even asking, Rod, a Christian businessman and a friend of the abbey's, offered to lend me one of his jackets. (I view him and his wife, Tess, as well as the few others who frequent the early morning prayer and Mass at the abbey as "regulars" or "habitués.")

Since I've come to know Rod more over the past couple of years, I did not feel at all shy to accept his offer. In fact, he had attended my abbey talks before, and he even enrolled the year before in "Soul Companioning," which is one of the eCourses we regularly offer through CenterQuest. It was so nice of him to even think about the jacket, which fit me quite comfortably (and served me well on many occasions, especially on cold mornings when I attended Lauds).

This morning, however, I could tell the moment I got out of bed that it was going to be a warm day. True enough, as noontime approached, it became almost unbearably hot and humid. By midafternoon, it was raining cats and dogs—the first heavy downpour I have witnessed during this visit to the abbey (and it would definitely not be the last). Luckily I had Rod's jacket to shield me from the raging torrents while crossing from one corridor to another on my way back to my room. By the time we started Vespers, the rain finally subsided and the whole place had drastically cooled down. The abbey grounds appeared so fresh and the entire surroundings seemed so clean and bright.

Afterward, in my email inbox I found a visual graphic from a friend in the US, with Hosea 6:3 superimposed, which I thought fitting to ponder after my experience of the rain. A case of divine synchronicity?

> *Let us know, let us press on*
> *to know the LORD;*
> *His appearing is as sure as the dawn;*
> *He will come to us like the showers,*
> *like the spring rains that*
> *water the earth.*

25 MARCH
wednesday

Annunciation

On this feast day of the Annunciation I received my own "announcement," once again from Facebook. Bob Holmes, who hosts the widely followed blog called *Contemplative Monk*, has always ministered deeply to my soul through the carefully picked wisdom quotes he posts every day. Today's post was both familiar and a very popular one, widely known as the "Prayer of Thomas Merton," a prayer I felt a strong impulse to claim as my own, and to use to pray to God—and I did, for it characterized the very longing of my heart during this time of stark uncertainties.

My Lord God,
I have no idea where I am going.
I do not see the road ahead of me.
I cannot know for certain where it will end.
Nor do I really know myself,
and the fact that I think I am following your will
does not mean that I am actually doing so.

But I believe that the desire to please you
does in fact please you.
And I hope I have that desire in all that I am doing.
I hope that I will never do anything apart
from that desire.
And I know that if I do this
you will lead me by the right road,
though I may know nothing about it.
Therefore will I trust you always
though I may seem to be lost
and in the shadow of death.
I will not fear, for you are ever with me,
and you will never leave me
to face my perils alone.

26 MARCH
thursday

Providential Connection?

A few days ago, I received a request from a representative of Paraclete Press to review a soon-to-be published work by Gabrielle Earnshaw, the Nouwen archivist, with whom I have come to be acquainted over the years through my own research on Henri Nouwen. I had originally meant to simply skim through the draft sent to me out of curiosity about the behind-the-scenes making of Nouwen's highly popular book *The Return of the Prodigal Son*. But I quickly found myself deeply engrossed in examining the advanced reader's copy for a good couple of hours. Now I have a fuller understanding of why this particular work of Nouwen holds such a special spot in many people's hearts, including mine (being the very first of Nouwen's books I had ever read). Kudos to Gabrielle for a splendid (and very thorough and thoughtful) documentation of the book's background, context, and enduring impact!

Right away I wanted to get back to Sr. Estelle, the author agent from Paraclete Press, to convey how much I enjoyed reading Gabrielle's work. While trying to compose my reply to her, I noticed as part of her signature panel at the bottom of her email a short quote from the Rule of St. Benedict. Naturally my curiosity was piqued, so I started clicking on the hyperlink to Paraclete Press. I learned that Sr. Estelle has been a sister at the Community of Jesus, a monastic community in the Benedictine tradition, and that Paraclete Press serves as the community's publishing arm. Of course, I was aware of Paraclete—it had published *The Seeking Heart: A Journey with Henri Nouwen*, written years ago by a fellow "Nouwenite" author and colleague, Charles Ringma. What had failed to register to me until now is that Paraclete represents, according to its website, "a full expression of Christian belief and practice—Catholic, evangelical, mainline Protestant, Orthodox—reflecting the ecumenical charism of the community and its dedication to sacred music, the fine arts, and the written word."

Of course, this description heartily resonates with me. Ever since I embarked on my most recent writing project—which was to be my first ever non-Nouwen book, with the working title *Quest for the Center: Exploring Our Spiritual Core*—I've been on the lookout for an ecumenical publisher, and Paraclete seems like one I should check out seriously. What's more, it has Benedictine spirituality at the heart of its identity—a definite plus for a Benedictine oblate like me!

Persuaded that it must be a providential connection, I wasted no time and contacted Paraclete's editor in chief, Jon Sweeney, with whom I found even more noteworthy connections. First, I knew of Jon through his 2008 book *Almost Catholic: An Appreciation of the History, Practice, & Mystery of Ancient Faith*, written when he was still an Episcopalian (he has since converted to Catholicism). The Philippines, it turned out, was familiar territory to him, for in his younger days as an evangelical, he served as a missionary in Batangas City on the island of Luzon. Furthermore, I learned that prior to moving to Paraclete Press, Jon cofounded and served as the editor in chief of SkyLight Paths Publishing, the company that published my fourth book on Nouwen, *Mere Spirituality: The Spiritual Life According to Henri Nouwen*.

✢ ✢ ✢

Less than a week later, I submitted my book proposal and sample chapters to Jon for his review. Now I am just waiting for Paraclete's final determination whether it's a good fit for their press. Naturally I have been coping with a mixture of anxiety and eager anticipation.

The Monk's Refectory

27 MARCH
friday

About Food and Snakes

Today Facebook reminded me through its "Memories" pop-up that two years ago around this time, I gave a series of Lenten Recollections to the monks, oblates, and guests of the abbey during Holy Week. I did the same last year, and I was supposed to continue the tradition this year, except that with the ban on group meetings, there is no way we can proceed with it. That said, I still felt resistant about the abbot's suggestion to push through with the modified plan of conducting my presentation exclusively for the monks.

✦ ✦ ✦

I knew I would have an early start today—sitting in on a Zoom session of one of our online classes for our CenterQuest School of Spiritual Direction (CQ SSD). I spent the remainder of my morning working to reschedule our next SSD cohort from October 2020 to January 2021 because of the pandemic. The extremely detailed process felt overwhelming.

Feeling exhausted and hungry, I must have devoured my biggest lunch since coming to the abbey.

After that, I could not imagine eating dinner. (I've always been self-conscious about gaining weight, so I have to deliberately watch it.) The abbey cook has been feeding me extra well, with all kinds of the freshest fish I've only tasted here in the Philippines. (*Lapu-lapu*, the king of all fish locally, remains my very favorite.) Not to mention the sweetest-tasting mangoes, unrivaled even in California.

I told Dom Carlo, who manages the guest house, that since I am the only one being served food there (the other two retreatants have left already), I didn't mind skipping dinner altogether. At first, I could tell he wasn't taking me seriously, for he could not imagine me not having dinner. I assured him that if I were hungry, I could eat some leftovers from the Refectory. I finally managed to convince him not to worry about me; in the US I have gotten used to eating only one main meal a day, which is lunch. (I am also used to doing intermittent fasting every now and then.) Besides, every feast day (of which there are many) I get invited to join the monks for dinner anyway.

The truth is, I rarely get hungry at night. For one, you can always expect morning and afternoon *merienda* (snacks). In the abbey (and everywhere else in the Philippines, for that matter), having two snacks per day (sometimes even three, including an evening snack) is a given—usually freshly baked bread rolls served warm from the Abbey Bakery, which I partake in once in a while—never mind that they are high in carbs! Every time I do, I make sure to drink my special turmeric-ginger tea (which I'd brought with me from the States) before ending my day, usually between 7:30 and 8 P.M. It's hard to believe that I am slowly acquiring the habit of retiring at around that time, like everyone else inside the cloister.

In the beginning, it felt slightly eerie to find the whole place already dark and silent so early every night. More often than not, I'm the only person walking through the long corridors inside the enclosure in the early evening. This didn't concern me until I made the mistake of asking a couple of the monks whether there'd been any snake sightings in the area. "Oh yes, of course," they confirmed—and not just your garden-variety kind but cobras. Apparently the monks have gotten used to the snakes and even refer to Fr. Elias, one of the four monastery priests, as their expert snake handler. People here have watched him pick up a snake, spin it around, and throw it as far as he can, to release it back to its natural habitat. The abbot even mentioned that he'd witnessed one snake slithering its way through what looked to me like a dry canal underneath the covered breezeway leading toward the sacristy.

Snakes are viewed in the monastery as uninvited but expected visitors, so much so that the monks are specifically instructed to keep their doors closed against these unwanted creatures. I regretted ever raising the subject of snakes; the very thought of them creeps me out completely.

✦ ✦ ✦

Almost every night coming from my office, I pass by the Refectory to fetch myself a cup of hot water for my turmeric-ginger tea ritual. Once in a while, instead of passing through the long corridors inside, I take the shortcut through the grassy patch outside. I don't mind the quick outdoor walk despite my mild night blindness. Crossing the stretch one night, I thought I had accidentally stepped on a snake; I literally jumped on the spot, only to realize it was just the water hose. Thank God I didn't scream and wake up the monks!

The next morning when I saw Pablita, the petite lady I regularly watch meticulously tending the abbey grounds, I was so tempted to call out to her and give her a piece of my mind for nearly scaring me to death by leaving the uncoiled hose lying on the ground overnight—but the more sensitive *Pinoy* (short for Filipino) in me prevailed and I didn't have the heart to say anything to her.

✧ ✧ ✧

Today also happens to be Dom Joaquin's birthday, but for some reason the community celebration is scheduled for tomorrow. As I have come to expect, I was invited to join the monks for dinner at the Refectory—which I have begun to look forward to as an opportunity to fellowship with everyone informally (to say nothing of another chance to break my Lenten sugar fast for the third time with the anticipated ice cream and cake for dessert).

28 MARCH
saturday

Of Zoom and Bells

This is the second day in a row that I have begun my day in the office sitting in on yet another Zoom session. Since 2013, when we first launched CenterQuest, which runs our School of Spiritual Direction hybrid program (a combination of residential and online learning modalities), Zoom has been our web conference tool of choice.

With the rise of the pandemic, a lot of Christian folks who used to be skeptical about using web and video-conferencing technology to make spiritual connections are now relying heavily on it for its convenience. Prior to the pandemic I was one of only a few people who frequently posted Zoom screenshots on Facebook, but now such screenshots have become commonplace on people's Facebook feeds. It's not surprising that many now also suffer from Zoom-fatigue syndrome. After "Zooming" for two consecutive mornings, I felt "Zoomed out," even though I am already accustomed to the platform.

After the call, I determined to get out of my office to catch some fresh air. It's so relaxing to walk around and take a few photos of the Abbey Church, especially with some of the most attractive bonsai trees in the foreground. Just looking at these miniature trees never fails to leave me wonderstruck, with all their intricate features majestically shot through with the divine.

This afternoon, after a good rest, I headed toward the main chapel to attend Vespers, and for some reason the imposing abbey bell tower caught my attention. The sight of church bell towers and carillons never ceases to fascinate me. Shipped all the way from Germany, I learned, these bells hanging high up in the tower were generously donated by Archabbot Notker Wolf, OSB, of St. Ottilien Archabbey.

I don't know what came over me in that moment—perhaps a wave of boredom was starting to hit—but I began imagining myself ringing those bells, with total abandon, by mightily pulling the ropes. To visually document my fantasy, I requested that Dom Arcadius, who was assigned that week to do the bell ringing ten minutes before the hour of five, take a souvenir picture with me vigorously tugging the bell rope.

Dom Arcadius is a very reserved and quiet monk who plucks his guitar every night in the dark during the 7 P.M. Compline (Night Prayer) at the chapel while the monks sing, in English, the old Latin hymn *Te Luces Ante Terminum* ("To Thee Before the Close of Day") in harmony. I have definitely fallen in love with its stirring melody and sublime lyrics, which are imbued with so much meaning that I often find myself automatically humming the tune on my way back to my room as I end the night.

Te Lucis Ante Terminum

*Now in the fading light of day
Maker of all, to you we pray*

That with your ever watchful love
You guide and keep us from above.

Help and defend us through the night
Danger and terror put to flight
Never let evil have its way
Preserve us for another day.

Father Almighty this be done
Through Jesus Christ, our Lord, your Son
Whom with the Spirit we adore
Who reigns with you forever more.
Amen.

It was so thoughtful of Dom Arcadius to provide me with the guitar chords for the song and, to my delight, to even bring his spare guitar (complete with a guitar stand) to my office—without me even asking him for it—and leave it there for me to use for my entire stay in the abbey.

I had not strummed a guitar for such a long time, and it was the perfect opportunity to relearn the familiar chords I used to play. I do this, every now and then, on my work breaks in the office.

I can't help but ask myself, "How has my life gotten so preoccupied that I lapsed this long from delighting in one of my most life-giving hobbies?" Maybe over time I have racked up too many convenient distractions—or even manufactured some of them—and they have subtly contributed to preventing me from accessing the more tender regions of myself.

Thank God It's Sunday!

It is Sunday, my favorite day of the week. But something is clearly missing from the scene. Gone is the Sunday crowd of habitués—blame it on the pandemic. The monks have unanimously decided—with the strong recommendation of Dom John Paul, a registered nurse in his juniorate formation—to exclude outsiders from Mass from now on. Aside from the Benedictine nuns—close to a dozen of them—who also join us every Monday, Wednesday, and Friday, all the morning Masses and daily observances of the liturgies (Lauds [Morning], Sext [Midday], Vespers [Evening], and Compline [Night]) are limited to the monks and me, the only layperson left inside the abbey.

The nuns are fondly referred to by the monks as the "Blue Sisters," since they switched from wearing their original black to blue habits. They are all from the Mary the Mother of the Church monastery close by, which occupies a parcel of land owned and donated by the abbey. This contemplative congregation originated in the town of Assisi, Italy, and settled in Malaybalay in 1995 at the invitation of Abbot Ed. Sr. Maribel and Sr. Virgie (who drove me to Cagayan de

Oro on March 16) remain part of this congregation, even after both of them have moved to Surigao City (about an eight-hour drive) and founded Monasterio de San Benito in September 2013—a monastic house sitting on a five-hectare plot of land donated by Sr. M's family, which I was originally supposed to visit before coming to the abbey.

Although they belong to a different branch within the Benedictine family, the Blue Sisters are very much a part of the abbey's community activities. I regularly see some of them after Mass, hand-delivering what I first thought were bottles of wine to Fr. Columbano. At eighty-three, Fr. Col, as we call him, is the oldest monk in the abbey and has been suffering from a colon tumor for about two years. I discovered later that these bottles actually contained a concoction boiled out of *camote* (sweet potato) tops that helps in the production of red blood cells.

Except for the fact that Fr. Col always moves about using his walker, I would never have known that he has cancer. He appears as healthy as anyone his age; he has a naturally sanguine disposition, is always upbeat, and wears a cheery smile.

While Fr. Col's overall demeanor hardly changed, his physical energy waned considerably in the weeks following. This Sunday Mass would be the last I would see him celebrate for the rest of my stay in the abbey. After that, only three other priests (Fr. Ed, Fr. Pachomius [Paco], and Fr. Elias) alternated standing behind the massive stone altar, which always captivated my visual attention.

I was so intrigued to know where this enormous rock could have come from that I had to ask the abbot about it. The monks happened upon it near the church during construction, and as they laid eyes on it, Abbot Ed became convinced that it would be a perfect center point for a church that was equally colossal in size. Under the supervision of Fr. Elias, the gigantic volcanic rock (estimated to weigh around twenty tons) was placed on a metal sheet and was pulled by bulldozer into the newly constructed church.

Now it has assumed the place of the grand altar—the attention-riveting block at the center, so distinct and unlike anything I have ever beheld in any other church. To me, this ceremonial stone calls to mind Psalm 118:22–24:

> *The stone that the builders rejected*
> *has become the chief cornerstone.*
> *This is the LORD's doing;*
> *it is marvelous in our eyes.*
> *This is the day that the LORD has made;*
> *let us rejoice and be glad in it.*

| The grand altar made of volcanic rock

✢ ✢ ✢

One of the reasons I always anticipate Sunday with much eagerness is that it has become my designated rest day, when I chill out and do nothing. Today I felt a tad agitated. I couldn't seem to erase from my mind the *New York Times* headline I read a few days earlier: "The U.S. Now Leads the World in Confirmed Coronavirus Cases," with a tagline that declared that "the nation is now the epicenter of the pandemic." This news upset me because I thought about home—or, to be more direct, the frightening possibility of not being able to go home. My mind ran wild as I envisioned what being stranded here would be like. I knew better than to nourish such an idea, so I resorted to what I've always done when plagued with such negative imaginings—walking around the cloister. The whole enclosure looked empty but tranquil, as if I were the only soul roaming inside the spacious monastery.

As I made my way through the various corridors, I couldn't resist photographing them, including the perfectly aligned concrete posts that projected an equally perfect overall perspective. All of a sudden, the cliché that "everything is a matter of perspective" rang true: I can view all that's been going on in the world as a curse, or I can choose to see this new reality—which I can't pretend to understand—through the lens of Providence. Yes, even divine Providence, and not in any way a coincidence or an accident.

Thank God it's Sunday!

> *Everything is a matter of perspective* 〞

30 MARCH
monday

Divine Couriers

Since the other morning, I've been trying to videotape myself addressing CenterQuest's target audience—our prospective School of Spiritual Direction applicants—to issue a major announcement of the change in the official start date of our fifth cohort from October 2020 to January 2021 because of the pandemic. I want the Abbey Church in the background to dramatize my being "providentially" stranded here. However, the harsh glare of the morning sun has interfered with my desired lighting for the video. The abbot suggested that I film it immediately after the 6 A.M. Mass today, before the sun has fully risen. To express his complete support for my project, he even excused Dom Pietro from attending Terce (the "third-hour" prayer observed in the abbey right after Mass, at around 6:15 A.M.) to assist me in my outdoor shoot.

Dom Pietro proved to be an able and patient assistant: moving the tall donation box from the chapel out to the lawn in front so I could rest my laptop there, shifting the box's position each time the fluctuating sunlight obstructed my video screen capture, and controlling the outside noise by signaling to folks at the nearby guardhouse to quiet down. After several takes, I finally got my desired footage and we wrapped up our morning.

Afterward, when I showed the video to the abbot, he chose the footage from the angle he thought best showcased the Abbey Church, with which I happened to agree. I was relieved to accomplish my first important project at the abbey; this has a large bearing on my ability to communicate to the outside world what I deem to be an urgent message concerning the future of our school amid the reality of our lockdown situation.

✢ ✢ ✢

At 8 A.M. I was back at my office ready for a Zoom meeting with a longtime directee from New York. As a music therapist working in a huge correctional facility in New York City, he told me that because of the recent coronavirus outbreak inside his workplace, he, along with some other employees, had been released from work temporarily. Feeling fatigued and having lost his sense of smell, he suspected that he might already be infected. A physically fit marathon runner in his early forties, he hadn't thought he would catch the virus, although most of his symptoms seemed to indicate otherwise.

"Wow, this is really happening—and to people I know personally," I said to myself, almost naively. I said a quick prayer for him before concluding our time together and instructed him to email me at once, whatever he found out. Sure enough, two days later he tested positive for COVID-19. I felt sorry for him (but thank God he survived it well and was back to his normal self the following month when we reconnected on Zoom). My spiritual direction session with this New Yorker on this particular

Monday sobered me and it got me wondering once again, "What in the world is happening in our time?"

✢ ✢ ✢

Before noon, I was informed by one of the women in the office next door that an LBC courier package addressed to "Dom Wil" had just arrived. I smiled, knowing it must be from Sr. M, whom I requested to secure some of the needed items I had failed to pick up before coming to the abbey. As I unwrapped the package I found several packets of hand wipes (I wondered why I would need that many since I'd only be here for a month—so I thought!), a couple of packets of Fisherman's Friend lozenges, and instead of the Berocca multivitamin tablets, which she said were sold out, a one-month supply of powdered Korean vitamin C, packaged in very tiny packets. (I later found out that this was part of Sr. M's family business.) The only thing missing was a bottle of hand sanitizer, which she said was impossible to find at that time. There was also an envelope containing a few thousand pesos, which she had exchanged for the American dollars I had given her before we parted ways on March 16 and which I was sure would be more than enough for any expenses I might incur during my short stay in the abbey. I texted Sr. M immediately to thank her and let her know that I received everything she sent in top condition—and much earlier than she had anticipated.

> **" What in the world is happening in our time?**

✢ ✢ ✢

As I was mindlessly scrolling through my Facebook feed this afternoon, God delivered a personal message to me, using two of my favorite Anglican theologians as divine "couriers"—what a treat! The first was a *Time* magazine article by the prolific British author and New Testament expert, N. T. Wright. The title itself and an excerpt from the article speak volumes about the situation we're all confronting:

Christianity Offers No Answers about the Coronavirus. It's Not Supposed To

Rationalists (including Christian rationalists) want explanations; Romantics (including Christian romantics) want to be given a sigh of relief. But perhaps what we need more than either is to recover the biblical tradition of lament.

The second message was a poignant quote from the theologian and former archbishop of Canterbury Rowan Williams, posted by the blog *Contemplative Monk* that has widely circulated on the internet:

People now have a painful need to be helped to be still. A church that is too noisy, too caught up in its own busyness, to answer this need is failing deeply.

As if they weren't enough to chew on during a Monday—the real beginning of my week—the clincher for the day came through my email inbox toward the end of my afternoon, from Joan Chittister's weekly *Vision and Viewpoint* e-newsletter. Her last paragraph dished out the punch line for me—what real transformative struggle entails in the thick of life's unwanted interruptions:

To struggle is to begin to see the world differently.
It tests all the faith in the goodness of God
that we have ever professed.
It requires audacity we did not know we had.
It demands a commitment to truth.
It tests our purity of heart.
It brings total metamorphosis of soul.
If we are willing to persevere
through the depths of struggle
we can emerge with conversion,
self-acceptance, endurance, faith, surrender,
and a kind of personal growth that takes us
beyond pain to understanding.
What we see is the fullness of the self come
to birth in the only way it really can:
in labor and under trial.

Chittister always helps me to grasp more clearly what I sense is taking place inside of me. I have been experiencing a personal homecoming of sorts—where scattered fragments of my broken self are slowly being integrated, enabling me to attain a wholeness of being. It's the quality of wholeness borne out of both inner and outer struggles so real that only genuine surrender can release their grip on me. For me, the core issue is one of control—my obsession to know, to grasp, to see things clearly. When these driving desires aren't met to my satisfaction, they can deeply unsettle me unless I decide to let go—a tough act. At the same time, I realize there's no other way to live but through the spirituality of struggle.

✦ ✦ ✦

Who would've thought that Facebook could actually be an invaluable vehicle to arrest one's distracted attention? All the more reason to defend myself against my youngest son David's biting charge that his dad is such a "social media fanatic"—his exaggerated perception of my overinvestment in Facebook.

But seriously, I never expected God to break open three consecutive messages (through God's "divine couriers") to me within a span of one day through my Facebook feed, jolting me out of my complacency when the situation around me became predictably unpredictable.

 There's no other way to live but only through a spirituality of struggle.

31 MARCH
tuesday

Praying the Hours

I've been in the abbey now for almost half a month and I have found myself gradually getting the hang of the monastic rhythm, which, on one hand, seems incalculably slow (compared to the pace I've been accustomed to) and, on the other, strangely fast-moving; the day was over before I knew it. Maybe this has to do with the cyclical and predictable rhythm of the *Horarium*, the monastic timetable for canonical prayers—also known as the Liturgy of the Hours, the Divine Office, or *Opus Dei* (Work of God).

As an oblate, I am conscious of the crucial importance of public and communal prayer (primarily consisting of chanting the psalms) for all Benedictines. The Rule of St. Benedict (RB) devotes no less than twelve chapters to addressing this. The very first paragraph of chapter 43 concludes: "Indeed nothing is to be preferred to the work of God"—referring to the disciplined practice of praying the hours as a way of cultivating ongoing awareness of God's presence. The Rule states categorically, "We believe that the divine presence is everywhere . . . but beyond the least doubt we should believe this to be especially true when we celebrate the divine office" (RB 19:1). Put simply, Benedictines believe we can consecrate each day of our lives in a "rhythm of remembrance," through well-structured times of intentional prayers—contemplative pauses that punctuate our day, reminiscent of the Psalmist's declaration, "Seven times a day do I praise you..." (Ps 119:164).

To Benedictines, praying the hours is one practical avenue for attending to our relationship with God and thus opening ourselves up to our continual renewal and conversion. I never quite understood what this actually meant until I experienced it myself in late 2004 while writing my doctoral dissertation for a protracted period of time at Saint Andrew's Abbey in Valyermo, California. At first, every time I heard the bell calling us to prayer, I would grudgingly inch my way to the chapel to join the monks—the least I could do to express my appreciation for their hospitality (a very Pinoy stance, I should say).

We believe that the divine presence is everywhere ... ""

But over time, the psalms started to sink into my consciousness, slowly but surely shifting many of my perspectives and convictions about my own spiritual journey. I knew for certain that God was using the words I kept hearing and repeating, day in and day out, to speak to my needs and concerns, consequently affecting my perception of reality. For instance, when feeling burdened by something, a specific psalm would flash through my mind at just the right time, surprising me with new insights on my present issue. As someone who had long resisted engaging in what I wrongly interpreted as mechanical prayer, this was a significant turnaround.

There was no question in my mind that I was being converted from the inside. Since that transformative experience at Saint Andrew's, I developed the daily habit of praying on my own quite consistently, at least morning and night prayers, following the liturgy guide on the osb.org and universalis.com sites.

Since becoming an oblate, I have had the good fortune to visit a number of Benedictine monasteries and abbeys in the United States and other parts of the world, conducting various retreats. Through this broad exposure, what has become evident to me is that each community has its own fixed way of going about its liturgy (even within the same Benedictine tradition).

Sometimes I've wished that all Benedictines would just adopt and follow one standard Breviary, or prayer book. Each time I visit a new place, I have to shift gears and reorient myself to the community's particular method of doing liturgy (chanting, singing, reciting, etc.). But then again, I suppose such diversified approaches allow each community to establish its unique identity.

The Abbey of the Transfiguration is no different in that it has clearly assumed its own definitive character and personality as a decidedly contemplative monastic community, exuding a certain ambience and subscribing to a particular ethos. Ever since I first visited the abbey in 2017, I have sensed a different feel in both the place and the community, but I couldn't pin down precisely what it was that made the community stand out for me.

Having stayed here for half a month now, I can point to their liturgy, among other things, as a definite draw for me, as well as the solemn, contemplative aura; the monks' chanting in perfect cadence; the organ music, both meditative and majestic; the four-part harmony singing; and the elegant rituals and ceremonies the abbey stages on special occasions.

My particular attraction to liturgy is one of the treasures I've recovered from my Catholic heritage, despite my meanderings into all sorts of contemporary worship expressions from various Christian traditions—nondenominational, interdenominational, and transdenominational; I have come to appreciate the legitimacy of variety in liturgical approaches. Yet over the past fifteen years or so, I've no longer been able to ignore my heart's deeper yearning for a more contemplative liturgy—the kind that always leaves me with a transcendent feeling of mystery and awe. I am reminded of Neil Postman's comment, which so resonates with me:

> The spectacle we find in true religions has as its purpose enchantment, not entertainment. The distinction is critical. By endowing things with magic, enchantment is the means through which we may gain access to sacredness. Entertainment is the means through which we distance ourselves from it.

This probably explains, in part, certain elements that draw me to the Episcopal "whistles, bells, and smells," and why elaborate Catholic rituals in general have always held a special space in my psyche, sending me back to childhood memories of processions, religious vestments, chants, incense, and stained glass windows.

Back to the Liturgy of the Hours: allow me to give a brief overview of the Divine Office as it is uniquely observed here at the Abbey of the Transfiguration. The monks begin their morning very early and gather for Matins (also known as the Office of Readings) at 3:40 A.M. in the Oratory, the small chapel inside the enclosure. Although there have been several occasions when I've been wide awake at 2 A.M., I have never attended Matins.

Lauds at 5 A.M. is my favorite, and I've rarely missed it. Except for feeling annoyed by the insects that hover around me in my pew, I always look forward to observing it. I love chanting the psalms and joining in the singing of the Benedictus (Canticle of Zechariah), usually cantored flawlessly by Fr. Paco. This is the personal highlight of the morning office for me. Mass immediately follows Lauds, and by 6:15 A.M., everyone proceeds from the main chapel to the Oratory for Terce, third-hour prayer, which is typically observed at 9 A.M. The monks do their Terce after morning Mass. I joined them for a few weeks until it became increasingly difficult for me because of my work demands. A short business meeting normally takes place after Terce, where the monks receive instructions for the day or any reminders from the abbot. There have been a few times where I've felt a bit awkward lingering during their meeting, and I've often wished to excuse myself, but no one, including the abbot, has ever made me feel like an outsider.

Everyone is back in the chapel by 11:30 for Sext, which goes by quickly, followed by noonday meal and an appointed reading. I don't recall ever joining the monks for lunch at the Refectory, but on several occasions at least one monk would join me for noon meal at the guest house. Rarely have I eaten there all by myself, as either the abbot or Dom Carlo is my regular "date," unless one of the other monks is "assigned" to keep me company. I have never participated in the office of None (Ninth Hour, or Midafternoon Prayer), which the monks here pray much earlier, at half past noon.

As with Lauds, I eagerly anticipate Vespers, and I always make sure to be on time, if not early. And similar to the Benedictus, I never cease to be moved each time Fr. Paco leads us in the Magnificat (Canticle of Mary). Little wonder that it didn't take me that long to memorize both canticles and the hauntingly melodic tunes. Once I asked Fr. Paco if he ever got tired of chanting the Benedictus and the Magnificat—I couldn't imagine myself doing these every day throughout every year. He said the routine has been so much a part of him for the past thirty-five years that it has become as natural as breathing.

The day before Solemnities, Vespers is followed by Vigils. Solemnities are celebrations of greatest liturgical importance and not to be confused with feast days, which are of secondary importance and each observed on a particular day of the year. Since Sundays are considered Solemnities, Vigils for Sunday take place every Saturday after Vespers.

Each evening is capped by Compline, which is conducted earlier than usual at the abbey—7 P.M. or sometimes even earlier, when the monks stay behind after Vespers for the Adoration of the Blessed Sacrament on Tuesdays and Fridays.

I never tire of singing the hymn "To Thee Before the Close of Day" every Compline, which the monks observe in darkness, with just one lit candle near the altar. This short service ends with singing the Marian antiphon *Regina Caeli* ("Queen of Heaven") as we face the image of Our Lady of Montserrat, positioned at the top-center wall, just behind the altar. Then we quietly depart from the chapel after the asperges, when the abbot blesses and sprinkles us with holy water.

✢ ✢ ✢

On a lighter note, the first time I heard the *Regina Caeli* (which is sung by the monks every day from Easter Sunday to Pentecost Sunday), two words got stuck in my mind because they rhymed and slightly tickled me inside. Not having studied Latin, the two words sounded to me like *resurexi* and *dixi*, which reminded me of the popular country singers the Dixie Chicks.

Later, I overcame my amusement when I checked the actual Latin texts for that particular line (*Resurrexit, sicut dixit*, meaning "has risen as he said"). Maybe I am just used to *Salve Regina* ("Hail, Holy Queen"), which is traditionally sung at Compline (from the Saturday before Trinity Sunday until the Friday before the first Sunday of Advent) and has become a personal favorite. I've practically memorized that hymn in Latin because my former oblate group in Burbank, California, always sang it after Compline, regardless of the liturgical season. I do miss singing the more familiar tune since I've been here.

Faith

April 1-30

"[Struggle] tests all the faith
in the goodness of God
that we have ever professed."

– JOAN CHITTISTER

1 APRIL
wednesday

A New Routine

The month of April has unceremoniously kicked in before I realized it—without the commonplace April Fool's pranks. (I am in an abbey after all!) Thus, the first of April has come and gone, almost unnoticed by most everyone—but not by me. I am starting to count the days and pay more attention to how each day will take shape and pan out.

Starting this week, Dom Carlo and I have agreed that instead of me having breakfast all by myself at the guest house, it would be much simpler if I just observed it at the Refectory with the monks, who normally have theirs anytime between 6:30 and 7:30 A.M. Since my daily schedule has taken on an entirely different flow than what I am accustomed to in the States, my own meal routine had likewise shifted considerably.

Whereas before, I would either just pick up an apple or take some seasonal fruit such as watermelon, pineapple, or strawberries for a late breakfast, or skip it completely (which was more often the case), now I have begun consistently having an early breakfast (since I began routinely skipping dinner). If I have a

Zoom or phone appointment (which has become a lot more frequent as the weeks pass by), I quickly grab a bowl of garlic brown rice and combine it with any of the abbey's staple fare: regular or spicy Spanish sardines, pickled and spicy tuna chunks, scrambled eggs with melted cheese inside (I love eggs cooked in every conceivable manner), or my ultimate pick, *tortang talong* (eggplant omelet), cooked in deep-fried egg with a slightly crispy texture.

I carry my breakfast bowl to my office and eat fast before starting Zoom, or sometimes even while on it. On days when I don't have early appointments, I join whoever happens to be in the Refectory (predictably three or four regulars). Aside from the regulars, I rarely encounter the other monks during breakfast; either they eat later in the morning or they fast, I presume. (Although I wouldn't be surprised if some of them actually went back to bed after the office of Terce to engage in *naptio divina* for a bit!)

✢ ✢ ✢

At 7:30 A.M., Fr. Paco graciously carved out some time from his busy schedule to give me a little tour of the St. Antony the Hermit Spiritual Center. This newly built site consists of dormitory rooms for private and group retreatants, a plenary session hall, an office space, and a small chapel still under construction—all made possible by a generous benefactor from the US.

Designed primarily to advance the contemplative ministry outreach of the abbey, this new facility is a welcome boost to the ongoing retreat work of Fr. Paco, who also heads up Heartspace, a meditation group he regularly facilitates both within the abbey and outside it, using the contemplative approach of John Main (Benedictine founder of the World

Community for Christian Meditation movement, or WCCM).

From there, we drove up the hill to the old monastery, where the abbey originally started. Except for the old chapel, which I saw briefly last year on my way out to the airport, I had never before had a chance to check out the various facilities, including a recently constructed addition—a multi-purpose building with four guest rooms. I did not realize how vast the property is.

With all the supervision of the construction sites and the ongoing facilities maintenance that Fr. Paco is in charge of, I no longer wonder why he seems so occupied; he has invested a lot of his energy into his heart's passion. Impressed with how the abbey has evolved over the years, and continues to do so, I am grateful and appreciative to Fr. Paco for this highly informative tour, which provided me a glimpse of the abbey's past and its future.

| The St. Antony the Hermit Spiritual Center

2 APRIL
thursday

Food and Fellowship

Every lunch hour I'm back at the guest house for my noon meal—the one big meal I partake of each day. The typical combination is a meat dish (chicken, pork, or beef) *and* (mind you, not "or") a variety of fish dishes (name it and I've probably tasted them all), some fresh veggies on the side, and seasonal fruit for dessert. Very seldom do I consume all of the generous servings; usually I leave one or two plastic-wrapped dish plates unopened. Often I feel guilt-stricken for not finishing everything. I am conscious of the fact that we're in the middle of a pandemic and there is, for sure, a scarcity of food in different places in the country. And yet as a true-blooded Pinoy, there is still a part of me that wants to exercise enough sensitivity to never give any impression to Manman, the cook, that I do not appreciate a particular dish that he has prepared so conscientiously for me. So there are times when I literally force myself to at least take a small bite of the food rather than leaving it untouched.

As if to assuage my feelings of guilt, both the abbot and Dom Carlo repeatedly remind me not to worry that the food would be wasted, since the guest house workers could always take home the leftovers. Despite their constant reassurance, I have to confess that I continue to be bothered by my consistent pattern of leaving unconsumed food on the meal table.

It hasn't taken long, however, for Manman to figure out that when it comes to his scrumptious garlic and buttered shrimp dish, I'll scrape everything off the plate. Once when I ran into him in the kitchen, I made sure, right there and then, to compliment him for the tasty shrimp he had concocted. I learned from Dom Carlo that Manman, who has been with the monastery kitchen since he was just a teenager (he's now in his midthirties), has always displayed a passion for cooking. Seeing his knack for it, Dom Carlo nurtured him by buying him cookbooks so he could keep experimenting with various dishes. Without a doubt, Manman is a natural cook, and I am fortunate to enjoy the blessings of his gift to the abbey.

Whenever the abbot is with me for lunch and the same shrimp dish is served—which I've noticed has become more frequent—he urges me to take his portion. Abbot Ed refuses to touch any kind of shrimp; he's definitely shown more discipline than I have by saying a flat no to certain foods that he and I are not supposed to indulge in. And I'm only too happy to oblige whenever he insists that I take his portion of the shrimp dish. I'm always quick to rationalize that this is what Allopurinol tablets are for: to regulate my uric acid level (and last I checked, I still had ample supply of them). Then I convince myself, for the nth time, that "it's only every once in a while" (which, of course, is no longer the case, since Manman keeps serving the irresistible dish).

✦ ✦ ✦

Dom Carlo has always made it a point to "assign" a monk to be with me during lunch; otherwise he ends up volunteering himself to keep me company. For the first couple of days this week, Fr. Col joined me. What a privilege it was for me to sit and listen to the abbey's oldest and most revered monk tell me all sorts of engrossing "war stories" about the early days of the monastery!

With razor-sharp memory—quite impressive for an eighty-three-year-old—he talks about the folks from all walks of life who have directly or indirectly been blessed by the abbey's presence or who have contributed in significant ways over the years to what the place has become now. I have the impression that not only does Fr. Col know a lot of people—both common folks and influential ones—but everybody seems to know him. Around the abbey and beyond, Fr. Col has surely been a well-loved figure—an institution, if you will!

Seeing how accommodating Fr. Col is as a person, with such jovial nature, I can't imagine what's not to like about him. Throughout our meal conversations together, he pours out story after story with his infectious enthusiasm. I have thoroughly enjoyed learning from this wise and seasoned monk, and I am lucky that I get to spend these brief but meaningful moments with him at the abbey.

3 APRIL
friday

A Quiet Place

Courtesy of the Mystic Prayers page on Facebook, I was greeted this morning by this quote from the late John O'Donohue, a famous Celtic spiritual writer:

You have been forced to enter empty time.
The desire that drove you has relinquished.
There is nothing else to do now but rest
and patiently learn to receive the self
you have forsaken in the race of days.

O'Donohue's penetrating words pricked my heart as I mused over them. During this "forced" period of spacious rest, there is indeed a deep longing stirring inside of me to come back home to myself, to the self that has of late become very preoccupied by seemingly endless demands vying for my already divided and scattered attention.

I had to shut my eyes for a while, to try and seize the moment and soak in the message. When I reopened them, the first thing I noticed was the guitar in the corner of the office. It was as though I was being lured right there and then to play the instrument that I had been reacquainting myself after a long time of not even touching it. My mind was brought back to a contemporary classic song by Ralph Carmichael entitled "A Quiet Place," and the next minute I picked up the guitar and started plucking it while I sang my way through this '70s favorite, surprised I still recalled the chords.

Not only was I lulled by nostalgic feelings while listening to myself sing the familiar lyrics of this cherished song, but I also felt rejuvenated as I allowed its well-timed message to sink deep into my soul. Still moved, I glanced through my office window and whispered to myself once again, "Thank you, God, for this 'quiet place' that you have appointed for me to treasure during this serendipitous period!"

4 APRIL
saturday

Reminded of God's "Wil"

Today, as well as yesterday, I had lunch with Dom Joaquin, one of a handful of monks with whom I became acquainted on my previous visits. Like Fr. Col, Dom Joaquin hails from the island of Bohol, and prior to becoming a monk he was on the faculty of Holy Name University in Tagbilaran City, teaching business for sixteen long years. Since entering the monastery, in addition to his other duties at the abbey, he has devoted his time to pastoral counseling, primarily for residential guests seeking spiritual accompaniment. With extensive experience in facilitating retreats and giving Recollections both within and outside the abbey, Dom Joaquin has ministered to a wide range of folks over the years: faculty, staff, and students of various schools; renewal groups; and lay ministers from local and neighboring regions such as Davao and Cagayan de Oro.

Last year, when I was giving talks during Holy Week here, Dom Joaquin sought me out for spiritual direction. I came to like him instantly because of his openness, but this time during our meals together I've sensed a feeling of discomfort in him, although I couldn't quite put my finger on it. It took him a while to warm up to me again and I wondered why.

Some time ago, I invited Dom Joaquin to participate along with Rod Llacer in an online class on soul companioning with our CenterQuest School of Spiritual Direction (CQ SSD). Despite some minor technical glitches and challenges, Dom Joaquin fared quite well, and it occurred to me to ask him to consider our fifteen-month SSD training program with cohort 5 starting in January 2021. As a Benedictine oblate, I so wanted Benedictine monks and sisters represented in our ecumenical school, especially in light of our vision to launch CQ-Asia in the future. I was always on the lookout for prospects to invite into our program, and Dom Joaquin seemed to me like a good candidate.

But the abbot, recognizing Dom Joaquin's natural leaning toward counseling and retreat-giving, encouraged him to consider theological studies at a seminary in Cagayan de Oro City. In preparation for this, Dom Joaquin is currently focusing on his prerequisite courses in philosophy at San Isidro College, a local school owned by the diocese. While not opposed to the idea of studying to become an ordained priest later, in obedience to the abbot, he's taking things a step at a time and continuing to discern where this new path may lead him.

In light of this, and in full support of Abbot Ed's vision for Dom Joaquin, I've had to give up the SSD idea for him. I would lie, though, if I didn't admit to a slight tinge of loss upon realizing that the SSD prospect was now clearly a closed door for him. Much as I had my own wonderful plan for Dom Joaquin—and I've been known to possess a strong vision for others and I'm not hesitant to express it—I knew in my heart I had to release him to pursue whatever God may have in store for him. I've had to come to terms with the fact that the tired jokes I always tell aren't working their magic this time—that is, "Where there's a Wil, there's always a way" and whatever I convey to people is tantamount to "God's perfect Wil!"

During my subsequent dialogue with him, I also sensed that Dom Joaquin is at peace with his present direction—reason enough for me to express my all-out support to him and to affirm the abbot's ministry path for him. After this ex-change, I felt Dom Joaquin slowly re-turn to his usual relaxed self with me.

> ❝ *Where there's a Wil, there's always a way*

And I can't help but wonder whether I've unconsciously been pressuring him unduly out of my own eagerness to enroll a Benedictine monk in our SSD program. I, too, have come to peace by gladly giving him up to God, and I can truly say that I pray for the best for Dom Joaquin.

✢ ✢ ✢

I spent the greater part of the afternoon quietly preparing for the short series of talks I will be shar-ing with the monks next week, Holy Week. (Yes, I finally ran out of excuses and gave in to the abbot's suggestion to do it exclusively for the community.) Later on, when I asked the assistants working in the accounting office to print some handouts for me, I discovered with some amusement that their little copy machine was just as contemplative as my day had been. The Brother printer was so painfully slow that I ended up hanging out in their office for much longer. I could only exclaim, "Oh, brother!"

5 APRIL
palm sunday

Under the Cloud of Unknowing

One of the festive features of Holy Week for me in the abbey is the Palm Sunday celebration. This Sunday, however, proved to be quite different in mood. For one thing, the general public is no longer allowed on the abbey premises, let alone inside the church. With the addition of the Blue Sisters, it was again just the monks and me in attendance at Mass. To be quite honest, this uneventful day was a total disappointment. I saw palm branches sitting on top of a table at the front of the church and that was it; I never even got to touch one.

It looks to me like the aura of my newfound "quiet place" will extend to the way the abbey ushers in Holy Week—in a decidedly low-key tone. Lowering my usual expectations, I braced myself for a much simpler, even quieter and trimmed-down observance (which in the past has always proven to be one of the highlights of my yearly visits to the abbey).

✥ ✥ ✥

And what a lousy way to end the day—by receiving an emailed advisory from Philippine Airlines (PAL) that my April 15 flight to Los Angeles has been cancelled, without any further explanation. My heart sank with this unwanted news. My mind automatically raced into calculation mode: It would be two more weeks before I could potentially leave the country. Assuming the lockdown would be lifted by the end of the month, I project that I should be able to fly out by May 1.

However, when I attempt to rebook my flight, the PAL website indicates that no flights would be scheduled until further notice. The fact that my domestic flight, from Cagayan to Manila with Cebu Pacific Air and also scheduled for April 15, has not been cancelled gives me some hope that the Manila lockdown will probably not extend beyond mid-April, as originally projected. If that is the case, then in all likelihood the existing ban for outgoing international flights might also be lifted.

Just the thought of such a prospect is enough to console me a bit. But I will make no further effort to rebook my international flight with PAL until I gain a better picture of the local situation in Manila. In light of multiple conflicting rumors around the issue of the lockdown—whether it would be extended or lifted by the government—the real story is anybody's guess.

Reality seems to be gradually but firmly inching its way into my system. It is becoming plain to me that beginning this Holy Week and onward, I suppose I'll have to get used to navigating each day under the "cloud of unknowing," which is tantamount to living in utter darkness. To say this is terribly unsettling would be a gross understatement.

Everyday Spirituality

We began this morning at exactly 8:30 A.M., the first of a three-part series on everyday spirituality. Although the abbot has made the gathering optional, to my satisfaction as well as the abbot's, almost everyone showed up at the small conference room—Fr. Col being an exception because of his health issues.

Dom Pietro had the slide projector and screen set up for my presentation. I knew this was going to be a much different setting than I was used to. Unlike previous talks, where I've addressed a good-sized crowd of abbey regulars, including a contingent of twelve or so oblates from Manila, now I am interacting more directly with an intimate audience of ten monks, including the abbot, on Benedictine spirituality, a subject matter in which I presume they are well-versed.

For this truncated series, I've chosen to focus on stability—one of the three core Benedictine values—and I've arranged my presentation into a three-point outline corresponding to each of the three days: centeredness, commitment, connectedness (the three Cs). The irony is that here I am speaking on the topic of centeredness while feeling very uncentered and distracted, especially in light of my recent flight cancellation and all its implications. On the other hand, I suppose my very current experience of the "instability of heart" also qualifies me to talk with conviction about what it means to be "ungrounded." The truth is, teaching on stability has boomeranged back to me on more than one occasion, pricking my conscience and convicting me.

Despite all this, I happily "survived" my first teaching day, with much consolation as my initial apprehensions soon vanished and most of the monks engaged freely with me on the topic, with the abbot himself helping facilitate an open discussion and exchange with his monks. Overall it was a great start!

The Monkhood of All Believers 🥟

After my talk, I hinted to Abbot Ed in passing that I should probably start donning a monk smock (like a work uniform), since I was already envisioning my potential "overstay" in the abbey because of the lockdown extension. At that, the abbot wasted no time to make it happen, right there and then, and requested one of the junior monks, Dom Jared, to run to his room and fetch a light-blue smock for me, which fit me perfectly. Being vested by no less than the abbot warranted a photo op, so he and I proudly posed for the camera, with the help of Dom Jared. Pleased to the core, I posted the picture on Facebook the next minute. I captioned it "The Monkhood of All Believers," referring to the title of a recently published book by my colleague and friend Greg Peters, who is an expert on medieval monasticism.

✧ ✧ ✧

Today, as on every first Monday of the month, the monks observed what they call "Hermit Day"—a free day for personal prayer and Recollection. After our gathering this morning, I didn't encounter most of the monks until Vespers.

| Abbot Ed with me wearing a monk's smock

7 APRIL
tuesday

Stability and "Forever"

My second morning presentation went favorably. Absent from our meeting was Dom John Paul, who alerted me beforehand that he was checking Fr. Col into the nearby hospital for a couple of days due to the presence of fresh blood in his stool, which lowered his hemoglobin level. Fr. Col ended up being transfused with one unit of red blood cell pack, while Dom John Paul stayed at the hospital with him.

I had lunch with Dom Jared both today and yesterday. I was surprised to learn that he attended my previous retreats and Recollections at the abbey, because I honestly don't remember him. Already in his midfifties—although he certainly didn't look it—Dom Jared, a highly extroverted and jolly soul, possessed a winning personality that instantly drew me to him. In fact, I am fascinated by his background, which he has relayed to me the last couple of days. Dom Jared left the Philippines in 2000 to work in the Chicago area as a computer programmer on an H1 visa. He became a US citizen in 2006. After a decade of working with three different companies in three different states, he requested that his final employer,

American Express, relocate him to the Philippines. Six months later, on St. Benedict's feast day on July 11, 2016, he resigned in order to explore the prospect of entering religious life.

Dom Jared was introduced to the abbey community through the late Fr. Sonny Ramirez, a well-known Dominican priest who founded *Barkadahan* (meaning "gang"), a Catholic youth organization based at the Santo Domingo Church, Quezon City, where he and Tess (Rod's wife) were members (they ended up reconnecting through the abbey after many years). Dom Jared just completed his novitiate period and professed his simple vows; he is now in the juniorate period as a formand, which, if he passes, will allow him to profess his solemn vows as a monk for life.

Very down-to-earth, yet retaining a spark of youthful idealism, Dom Jared speaks glowingly about the abbey as a paradise in which he pledges to stay forever. I must admit that whenever I hear anyone invoke the word *forever*, especially in a casual tone, the cynical side of me is quick to react with a "Yeah, right!" attitude. Dom Jared, though, far from being casual about it, declares his unflinching commitment to his vocation with the faith of a child and a firmness that leaves me in awe—to the point of feeling shame for almost giving in to my initial dismissive stance.

Without ever diminishing his optimistic outlook, Dom Jared has freely bared to me his hopes, long-ings, and even some of the challenges with living in community. While remaining open and transparent, I can sense the dynamic restraint he is deliberately exercising in recognition of his place as a formand. The few times we have interacted have profoundly impressed upon me the genuine devotion monks are willing to give to God and the community to which they choose to belong. I have truly come to appreciate these opportunities to get to know the monks one by one—some in more intimate ways than others—and to be blessed in the process. What a rare chance this has been for me!

8 APRIL
wednesday

The Real Culprit

My day began very early. I purposely got up before 3:30 A.M. to connect with Bo Karen Lee, the author with whom I've been wanting to touch base; she requested that we talk at 3:30 P.M. Eastern Standard Time. I set myself up in a room close to the Oratory, thinking that the Wi-Fi signal there would be stronger than the one in my office. This turned out not to be the case; Bo was straining to hear me, so I had to amplify my voice to the maximum, completely oblivious of the monks' observance of Matins nearby.

Later in the morning, after delivering my last talk to the monks, I encountered Abbot Ed, who complimented me on being such a diligent and serious worker who began my day so early, already on the phone doing business. Puzzled that he seemed so aware, I pressed him further how he knew: "Of course the whole monastery knew because we all overheard your phone conversation while we were in the middle of prayer." I was so shamefaced that I felt like apologizing to every single monk I met throughout the rest of the day.

Blame it all on the Wi-Fi—the real culprit!

Having my much-needed haircut |

9 APRIL
maundy thursday

Hair Day

After three consecutive morning sessions with the monks and the intense discussions that followed, I felt elated it was finally over yesterday. The abbot expressed his sincere appreciation for what he deemed to be a very fruitful community interaction, time well spent. I, too, was generally satisfied with the proceedings and honestly felt it was the least I could do for the community that has adopted me into their fold.

Now without anything hanging over my head—except my noticeably overgrown hair—I wanted to venture into something different this day, for a change, until I overheard some of the monks talking about having their hair cut. There is a local barber who trims the monks' hair, including the abbot's (who really doesn't have much to begin with), every two weeks or so. "What impeccable timing!" I said to myself. Without hesitation, I asked the abbot if I could insert myself into the schedule, to which he agreed in a jiffy, much to my joy.

So there I was, sitting at the end of an open corridor inside the monastery enclosure, wearing a bright pink gown—of all colors!—and entrusting my hair to Roan, the barber. Actually, I couldn't care less about the outcome; I just wanted a haircut, period!

Once my hair was trimmed, I desperately wanted to dye it, since all of the gray areas were on full display (not that any of the monks cared). When I showed my exposed gray hair to the abbot in his room, he was quick to pick up the hint and offered one of his Bigen hair dyes—to my surprise, he had quite a few stacked in his drawer. At first I felt guilty, but then I thought he could probably spare a box—after all, he didn't need much for his own hair!

✢ ✢ ✢

At 6 P.M., we gathered in the chapel for the Mass of the Lord's Supper, officiated by the abbot, without the typical foot washing ritual. Neither did we observe the usual procession of the Blessed Sacrament, nor the altar of repose. Because of the pandemic, both the Vatican and the Bishops Conference of the Philippines deemed it best to simplify the Holy Week liturgy to avoid any potential infections from occuring.

good friday

A Historical Encounter

After Lauds this morning, I joined the monks for the Stations of the Cross, led by the abbot. Just like the Rosary my family prayed every night when my grandparents were still alive, I did the Stations countless times, until I got tired of it and completely abandoned this mechanical practice, only to rediscover the rich significance of this ritual many years later, ironically as a converted Protestant. As I think about it now, my whole observance of Lent and all its associated rituals has continued to have new meaning for me.

When the Stations prayers were over, Abbot Ed pulled me aside and invited me to sit with him by the stone chair, near the foot of the bell tower. For the next half hour or so, he gave me a blow-by-blow account of the abbey's long and captivating history, which I will attempt to summarize here.

Abbot Ed was the abbot of the Abbey of Our Lady of Montserrat in Manila for six years (1980–1986) when he caught a vision to start a contemplative community whose main thrust was to build a center for spirituality. The island of Mindanao was chosen to be the prospective site for the monastic foundation, since it was there, in the province of Surigao, that the first Benedictine monks—from Montserrat Abbey in Barcelona, Spain—took over the mission territories previously occupied by the Society of Jesus in 1895. (The year 2020 marked the 125th anniversary of the presence of the Benedictine monks in the Philippines.)

A survey team was immediately organized, headed by Abbot Ed. Fr. Col was also part of the team, since he spoke the major language of Mindanao (Visayan). When they finally settled on the present site, Abbot Ed asked Fr. Col to consider staying in Malaybalay to ensure that their new foundation would be sustained through his continued presence. Fr. Col gladly obeyed and left his job as the alumni moderator of San Beda College in Manila to permanently relocate to Mindanao.

In 1982, the Council of the Abbot President in Rome approved the canonical erection of the Monastery of the Transfiguration in Malaybalay, Bukidnon, and allowed Abbot Ed to reside there from 1983 to 1986 to oversee the new foundation. The Council of the Abbot President also appointed a prior-delegate for the Manila Abbey, to serve in Abbot Ed's absence. When the monastery was officially declared an independent community from the abbey in Manila in 1986, Abbot Ed resigned as abbot of the Manila community and became the superior (prior) of the new monastery, with Fr. Col as his subprior.

Abbot Ed left the monastery in 2000 to undergo open-heart surgery, and a prior was elected in his place. After his recovery, the abbot served as assistant secretary of the papal nuncio at the Apostolic Nunciature in Manila (the Vatican Embassy) for fourteen years, while also teaching part-time at the Loyola School of Theology in the area of spirituality. When the Monastery of the Transfiguration was elevated to the status of an abbey in 2017, the community elected him as their very first abbot.

Of course, in Abbot Ed's chronicling of the events leading up to his own return to the abbey, he included many absorbing details of flawed and struggling people in all their unvarnished humanity—including himself. I came away from the conversation both fascinated and grateful for the privilege of witnessing the abbot's naked heart: he was so open and transparent about his own struggles, joys, triumphs, shortcomings, frustrations, disappointments, regrets, and heartfelt longings and desires as an abbot. He closed with a firm pronouncement that the Abbey of the Transfiguration was the community in which he wanted to spend the rest of his life.

> **" Every monastic community is still very much a human enterprise— yet divinely ordained . . .**

As someone whose first book dealt with a spirituality of imperfection, as embodied by my patron saint Henri Nouwen, I wasn't taken aback by any of the human stories the abbot revealed to me. In fact, through the abbot's narrative I've been able to catch wonderful glimpses of the sacramental blessings emerging out of the ever-present reality of human woundedness and the brokenness of our world. If anything, this informal but intense chat has served as a sobering reminder that every monastic community is still very much a human enterprise—yet divinely ordained and thus providentially guided by God.

✦ ✦ ✦

This afternoon, starting at 3 P.M., I participated in the typical Good Friday liturgy, featuring the Passion, ably read by Fr. Paco, Dom Carlo, and Dom Joaquin. It stood out to me that all three monks are endowed with good speaking voices. Listening to them enunciate their designated parts with conviction allowed me to receive the all-too-familiar Passion narrative with a fresher and deeper heart connection.

11 APRIL
black saturday

How Long, O Lord?

*At its core, contemplation
is the practice of openness
to the flow of the present moment.*

Thanks to David Benner, the well-known author and one of the members of our CenterQuest Board of Reference, for posting this wisdom quote on Facebook—one that I hope will provide me with a much-needed perspective to sustain me for the weekend. To be a true contemplative, Benner explains, is to be open to how the present moment unfolds. "OK, on this Black Saturday, I will do my best to be a good contemplative," I promise myself.

No sooner had I set out to go with the flow than I found myself derailed by a text message from my youngest son, David. Ever since my family learned a few days ago that my return flight to the States was cancelled, they have been conveying their mounting concern for me, particularly my two sons, Jonathan and David.

The other day, in a benign attempt to divert their attention away from me, I inquired how they were coping with the COVID-19 situation in California. In response came a text from David this morning: he and Christy, his fiancée, have decided to postpone their much-anticipated wedding, scheduled for July 4. I can only imagine their disappointment, knowing how extensively they've been preparing.

"Oh well, surprise!" I told myself silently, even as I added the news of yet another postponement to a list that seems to be getting longer by the day (like my own postponed retreats, classes, conference events, etc.). Later today I learned through my friend Leeboy, who booked my domestic flight to Manila, that my Cebu Pacific flight on April 15 will most likely be cancelled, as the airline's website already implies. Today, whatever remaining hope I had for flying out of Manila to the States next month just got snuffed out. In my simplistic thinking, the status of my domestic flight would determine the status of my international one. Now I can't even project when to rebook my flight to Los Angeles.

In the afternoon, still feeling distraught, I dragged myself to the chapel to attend the 6:30 P.M. Easter Vigil. As I walked, I came unglued inside. I was disappointed in myself for my epic failure to be the true contemplative I promised to be at the start of the day and for my utter inability to embrace the present moment, which, in my shortsightedness, I interpreted as nothing but an endless series of unwelcome events.

As I began climbing the brick-and-stone church steps, I lamented my situation—or should I say, my perceived situation, which by every measure I had completely blown up in my mind—silently complaining to God, "How long, O Lord?" Unquestionably I had gone overboard, but it felt great to release the tension that had built up inside of me.

By the time the Easter Vigil was about to begin, I'd already let out all of my pent-up frustrations before God and decided in my heart not to allow the earlier events of the day to rob me of enjoying the most celebrated event of the liturgical year, pointing to the Resurrection of Jesus. Despite this year's celebration being rather intimate with just the monks and the nuns, everything I have come to expect of the Great Vigil proceeded as usual: the blessing and the lighting of the paschal candle in total darkness; the lighting of our small candles; Fr. Paco's chanting of the *Exsultet* (Easter Proclamation); the Liturgy of the Word and singing of the *Gloria in Excelsis Deo*, including the Alleluia; the renewal of our baptismal vows; the sprinkling of baptismal water; and finally, the Liturgy of the Eucharist.

As I made my way out of the church and back into the enclosure, I could sense my burdens lifting completely. To privately celebrate my personal victory, I thought about the frozen dessert I'd prepared yesterday. Dom Jared had given me an avocado, which he picked from the tree behind the Oratory and which I turned into a dessert by mashing it, mixing it with whipped cream and condensed milk, then pouring everything into a mug and putting it in the freezer. Now I was excited to taste what I had concocted. All by myself, in the dimly lit corner by the kitchen sink, I finished my mug of creamy avocado, feeling so light inside my heart—but heavy inside my stomach—and called it a night!

12 APRIL
easter sunday

An Ache to Remember

Easter morning began with lots of Alleluia-singing, starting at Lauds, which signals the Eastertide season being ushered in. Easter Mass followed immediately, with the same few people in attendance as during the Great Vigil last night, causing the abbot to exclaim to me afterward, "This is the first time I've seen anything like this happen in all of my years here in the abbey!" Indeed, it is nothing I have ever imagined Easter to be like—all because of the bleak reality of the coronavirus pandemic.

> *It is nothing I have ever imagined Easter to be like—all because of the bleak reality of the pandemic.*

During dinner I joined the monks at the Refectory in celebration of Easter and, as expected, there was plenty of food on the table. To my sheer delight, there were also at least three different flavors of ice cream served for dessert, including one of my choice Pinoy flavors: *ube-queso* (purple yam with cheese). Easter Sunday is when I was supposed to end my sweets fast (although I actually ended it last night when I ate my frozen creamy avocado in secret). Already accustomed to not having dinner, I ate very little but feasted on a ton of ice cream instead.

In the middle of the night, I woke up with a nagging toothache that lasted almost five hours. I was well aware of a cavity in my molar, even before leaving the States in January, but I didn't have time to see my dentist. I figured I could easily have it fixed as soon as I returned to California, since it wasn't really bothering me at all—until I ate all that ice cream. Well, I paid for it, big time! The pain became almost intolerable, so much so that I was tempted to knock on Dom John Paul's door to beg for any pain reliever, except it was such an unholy hour and I had no idea which room he was staying in. Mightily, I prayed my way through the night until I fell back to sleep and the pain was gone when I got up in the morning—Hallelujah!

13 APRIL
monday

Home Away from Home

As soon as I received the official email from Cebu Pacific Air about the cancellation of my April 15 flight to Manila, I had Leeboy rebook it for May 1, first thing in the morning, just to be sure I had a spot reserved. It was crucial to get to Manila first, where the rest of my things were waiting in Parañaque with the Companions of the Redeemer guys with whom I was staying before my trip to Mindanao. I actually had three suitcases and a couple of boxes there. On top of that, I had a bunch of clothes, shoes, retreat materials, and some *pasalubong* (souvenir gifts) designated for my family and friends in the US.

I had originally planned to arrive from my Mindanao trip at least a day earlier and spend the night at the Companions of the Redeemer place to unpack and repack for my return flight to the US the following day. I imagined the one-day turnaround would be more than sufficient for me to sort out all of my stuff—what to bring back to the States and what to leave behind or give away. Or I could manage a quick turnaround on the same day, arriving domestically in Manila in the morning and flying out internationally in the evening, giving me at least a few hours of last-minute packing time. Synchronizing the schedule of my two flights was the challenge. It would've been far simpler if I were originating straight from Manila, but such wasn't the case; I had to get to Manila first and pick up my stuff before flying out of the country. Therein lay the potential complications that continued to cause me anxiety.

⁜ ⁜ ⁜

This morning I finally got the chance to post the abbey video I made before Holy Week on several social media sites—Facebook, LinkedIn, Twitter, Constant Contact, and our CenterQuest website— updating people about our new dates for cohort 5 of our CenterQuest School of Spiritual Direction (CQ SSD). I also sent out a few emails informing our target group of prospective SSD applicants about this important change. Fortunately, the first twelve early-bird applicants, who have already been accepted, are all OK with the new dates. But I'm still a bit anxious about how this announcement will affect our continuing recruitment process.

> *We shouldn't allow this air of uncertainty to deter us from what . . . God has called CenterQuest to do.* "

In the back of my mind, I know that moving the start date from the original October 2020 to January 2021 is no guarantee in terms of our goal of filling thirty spots—again, thanks to the pandemic! In my heart I am convinced that we shouldn't allow this air of uncertainty to deter us from what we feel God has called CenterQuest to do. With the full backing of our CQ team, I've done what I had to do and I am leaving the results to God. Getting this announcement out took up most of my morning. But I feel peace inside having done it. And there's no turning back now!

✥ ✥ ✥

To relax my mind a bit after such an intense morning, I occupied myself by taking many pictures—from every conceivable angle—of the centrally located Abbey Church, the focal point of the monastery. There's something magnetizing about this perfectly square church, with its minimalist design, pyramid motif, and imposing structure elevated on a hilly section of the monastery grounds. Each time I look at it, whether from afar or up close, it never fails to leave me in awe. At the same time, I feel this wonderful sense of at-homeness being around and inside this sanctuary. Later I posted select shots of it on Facebook with the caption, "My Abbey Home Away from Home."

The abbey's landmark feature

✢ ✢ ✢

Before resting in the afternoon, I passed by my office and found a booklet entitled *The Life and Miracles of St. Benedict* on the table, left there by Dom Jared for me to read. While starting to skim it, my attention was redirected to a few pages of handouts that went with the booklet dealing with the subject "Why Do We Have to Adore Before the Blessed Sacrament?" It got me thinking why Dom Jared wanted me to read it in the first place.

I couldn't help wondering if he was hinting at something. Was he curious about whether I was observing the Adoration of the Blessed Sacrament every Tuesday and Friday? And why would he even care? Perhaps he recalled the passing remarks I made publicly about my Catholic past and my Protestant present during a weekend retreat I conducted at the abbey some three years ago, which I didn't even realize he had attended. Was Dom Jared wanting to orient me to the significance of the practice?

Growing up Catholic, I've always been familiar with the Adoration ritual, including the Exposition and Benediction of the Blessed Sacrament service, which never failed to evoke in me a sense of reverential awe, even though I never quite understood it completely. I have to confess, it's only been fairly recently that I started revisiting the practice and have slowly begun to grasp its importance. Dom Jared's pamphlet was a welcome review.

About a year ago, I got to watch Bishop Robert Barron's video series on the Mass, which convinced me once and for all why I couldn't ignore my Catholic pull. Despite the mystery of the Eucharist and my utter inability to fully explain the doctrine of real presence (the belief that Jesus is literally present in the bread and wine, not merely symbolically), I know in my heart that the Eucharist has always been and continues to be the spiritual food and drink that deeply nourish my soul. (This is in sharp contrast to my former conditioning as a Baptist, where we embraced the opposite idea of "real absence," since the Eucharist is only reckoned as a memorial celebration.)

> " *The Eucharist . . . continues to be the spiritual food and drink that deeply nourish my soul.*

With a gnawing feeling of self-consciousness, it suddenly occurred to me to ask myself, "Did all the monks in this abbey have any idea of my faith journey?" More to the point, "Was Abbot Ed even aware of where I was coming from, or did everybody simply assume I was completely one of them?" I was forced to ponder, "Why would this matter to me at this time, and should it matter?"

The more I think about it, the harder it is for me to deny that the Protestant/Catholic split is still a very raw issue for me. Dom Jared's pamphlet simply brings into focus what I may be unconsciously avoiding dealing with. Without allowing this whole issue to dominate my thinking, I still deem it wise to continue my own ponderings but to treat them rather loosely instead of rigidly.

"Bonsai Beauty"

14 APRIL
tuesday

Bonsai Beauty

The sliding glass windows in my office encompass the entire length of the room I occupy in the abbey's main office building. So it is effortless for me to glance outside, overlooking the vast front of the Abbey Church. I could conveniently watch everything happening outside if I want to, and I do so every now and then just to break my routine a bit.

The one monk who has become almost a permanent fixture on the horizon is Fr. Elias, in his customary mode—watering the bonsai trees. These bonsai are splendidly positioned on both sides of the church steps, looking like landscaped mini terraces. Some are lined up elegantly across the railings of the wheelchair-accessible cemented path. There is no question that the bonsai collection is a majestic sight that dresses up the otherwise bare gray brick steps leading up to the main chapel.

It doesn't take a rocket scientist to conclude that the rare trees must be a very expensive collection. This was the first thing that caught the attention of my good friend Jeanne Chua when I brought her and her husband, Lowry, to the abbey last year. She owned a few bonsai, which used to be on display on the patio of their penthouse in Greenhills (Metro Manila), where I've often stayed when I am in their area. Jeanne couldn't believe her eyes upon seeing the massive collection around the abbey. (There are a choice few on the side of the church just before you enter the monastic enclosure, and some medium-sized trees at the center of the courtyard inside the enclosure.)

The first time I set foot in the abbey three years ago, I was told that these bonsai were all donated, but I never knew the whole story until this time, when I could no longer contain my curiosity, especially after taking countless photos of them. My friends who have viewed the photos on Facebook are in awe of the plants' splendor and exquisite detail. So one day I approached Fr. Elias and asked him for the details of the bonsai acquisition.

It all began when the abbot asked him if he could do something about the ornamental plants in front of the chapel, which were at odds with the simple but elegant design of the church. Tasked with redesigning this landscape, he breathed a prayer to God and wished that he could "make a rock garden with bonsai trees," and God heard his prayer. Eventually he was introduced to a bonsai master from Iligan City (about a four-hour drive from the abbey), who expressed his willingness to donate some of his choice collection as his way of leaving a bonsai legacy to the abbey before he passed away. Juvin Ignatius Dulay, the bonsai master who used to be the president of the Iligan Bonsai Society and who was the founder of *Bukas-Loob sa Diyos* (Open Heart to God) Catholic Charismatic Community, only stipulated that Fr. Elias take good care of them.

Fr. Elias had to learn the art of carefully pruning and meticulously rewiring the delicate miniature trees. A natural artist with good aesthetic sense, he started pouring his heart and energy into his newfound "babies," and treated each of them with tender loving care. The dedicated attention he continues to give to his bonsai never ceases to impress me.

> *I reckon it tantamount to a sin to fail to acknowledge the very presence of God in the face of such resplendent beauty.*

This afternoon I devoted a big chunk of my time to capturing, in still pictures, what I call the "bonsai beauty." I felt compelled to visually document their distinctive allure, and I must say, I am quite proud of the series of shots I took today. As an artistic person myself, I reckon it tantamount to a sin to fail to acknowledge the very presence of God in the face of such resplendent beauty. Spending unhurried time simply admiring the tangible manifestations of God's creative mind, evident in these intricate bonsai creations, is more than enough to make my day and carry me through yet another one.

Elegant bonsai trees adorning the front of the church

15 APRIL
wednesday

Losses and Gains

Indeed, God has faithfully carried me through this day, even as I mulled over the sobering reality that I was supposed to leave Mindanao and fly back to the US today. As a countermeasure to the disappointment still lurking inside me, I consoled myself with the thought that I was stuck in a safe, protected place where there were zero cases of covid-19 and I wasn't in a precarious situation where I wouldn't be sure what to expect (such as being in Manila, where the virus infection is escalating). Yet I couldn't deny how unsettled I felt in the face of these unpredictable conditions.

By now I've become acutely aware of the emotional roller coaster ride I've been experiencing lately, where I feel good one day and bad the next, or sometimes even contemporaneously. Henri Nouwen was right, after all, in claiming that both realities can coexist—a tensional phenomenon that we all need to learn how to navigate creatively.

What most people don't understand is that I've been gone ever since January, and to be caught in the possibility of yet another extended time away from home is very much disquieting to me. Of course, it may well be that I am flat-out homesick; I simply long to be back home. Period!

✣ ✣ ✣

We had light rain this afternoon. I normally don't like the rain; more often than not, it sets off melancholy in me. Today, though, I welcomed the rain. For the first time in a long time I saw both the positive and the negative sides of it, just as I can mourn my losses while at the same time celebrate my gains in life. With Job, I can now proclaim with deeper conviction, "God gives, God takes. God's name be ever blessed!" (Job 1:21, *The Message*)

16 APRIL
thursday

Discovering Vita Coco

This morning I came across an arresting article posted online by *Christianity Today* entitled "On Christians Spreading Corona Conspiracies: Gullibility Is Not a Spiritual Gift." With everything that's been going on in our world, some people seem to possess a keen sense of "rumor" and are determined to make our already troubled situation even worse by stirring up controversial theories about the current pandemic that even well-meaning Christians are subscribing to, rather naively. My Facebook Messenger is becoming cluttered with forwarded links to YouTube videos featuring all sorts of conspiracy theories that I do not care one whit about. I either ignore them or immediately delete them.

✢ ✢ ✢

This afternoon until the evening was exceptionally warm. During such days, the heat can prove punishing. At Vespers I felt sticky because of the high humidity, and those pesky mosquitoes were all over me. I picked up a thin liturgy pamphlet from the pew to fan myself throughout the prayer time, and I ended up using it to smack those blood-thirsty mosquitoes. I must've made some noticeable sound for I saw a couple of monks throwing hard-to-interpret glances at me. After that episode, I tried to be a little more discreet about my dealings with those annoying insects, which seem to be obsessed with my "stateside" blood.

✢ ✢ ✢

On my way back to my room after Compline, still feeling uncomfortably warm, I suddenly remembered the Vita Coco (a brand of coconut water) drink that Dom Joaquin told me about. I was informed that a bunch of them were stocked in the mini fridge just outside of Fr. Col's room. I heard that one of the owners of Vita Coco, who happened to be a good friend of the abbot's, donated a huge supply for the abbey's consumption. Without thinking twice, I headed straight toward the fridge and the top section was indeed full of them. When I noticed that there were even some packs stored on the movable shelf directly underneath the freezer, I grabbed myself an ice-cold pack and drank it quickly to cool myself off. It wasn't the most fresh-tasting coconut drink I've ever sampled but certainly thirst-quenching—and yes, it had this self-cooling effect on my system. From that day on, I became a frequent visitor to that fridge, especially on unbearably hot days.

17 APRIL
friday

The Magic of Lemon

My ever-faithful daily Facebook "companion" (obviously possessed with a highly computerized mind of its own) reminded me this morning, through its Memories prompter, that on this day last year, the abbey oblates—a considerable number of whom come from Manila—celebrated their renewal of vows. Many of these folks have become friends, and whenever I teach at Loyola School of Theology in Quezon City, I stop by their Thursday Oblates meeting nearby and join them for prayer—and, of course, for food, since we enjoy practicing *"ora eat labora"* together!

Gazing at their pictures on Facebook, I miss seeing their familiar faces here in the abbey this year. Months beforehand, we elaborately tried to coordinate our trips to the abbey via our Abbey Group messaging on Facebook. However, they had no choice but to cancel their much-anticipated annual trip to the abbey because of the lockdown in Manila. We were all disappointed. Too bad we can't all be together here. I can only imagine how they must have felt since they've never missed coming to the abbey for the last twenty-plus years. Thanks to Facebook, a number of them were able to keep regular track of my adventures here through my daily posts (and I could only imagine many of them were green with envy).

✧ ✧ ✧

For the most part, I used up my morning today Zooming—doing spiritual direction, chatting, coordinating with folks on some work-related projects. Really, if you don't watch it, you can easily succumb to Zoom-fatigue syndrome after a while.

✧ ✧ ✧

Later in the day, when I made my regular stop for my daily fix of ice-cold Vita Coco, I took notice of the several pieces of lemon on the egg shelf. I concluded they must be Abbot Ed's because on a previous visit I talked him into trying out the magic of lemon when he complained about his joint pains. After being sold on the benefits of drinking warm water with freshly squeezed lemon every morning, I overheard him ordering Dom Carlo to have Dom Diego, the marketer, buy some next time he went to the town market.

Drinking water with lemon each morning has always been part of my routine, until it was interrupted once I embarked on my Asian travels beginning last January. In the Philippines, it's been a little difficult (and pricey) to get lemons at times. Maybe next time I'll have the guts to ask for some from Abbot Ed.

18 APRIL
saturday

A Lemon Mix-Up

I've become a lot more at home with Abbot Ed since I arrived at the abbey. Feeling confident that I could ask him for anything, I approached him right after Mass this morning, just before I darted off to my office for another early Zoom meeting, and I boldly asked him if I could have one of his lemons from the refrigerator. "Why, of course!" he immediately replied (precisely the answer I expected). He indicated that I could take however many I wanted, anytime—yes!

I didn't hesitate to take him up on that, and since then I have gotten into the habit of passing by Fr. Col's room every other day after Mass to get my lemon supply from the fridge. I always cut the lemon in half, so it can serve me two days in a row. As has been my ritual back in the States, I squeeze one-half piece of the lemon into a mug of lukewarm water and mix in two teaspoons of apple cider vinegar—yes, to my delight the Refectory has the original Bragg's organic apple cider vinegar. On several occasions I've bumped into Dom Symeon, the abbey prior, heading in the same direction on his way back to his room.

Sometimes I even walk with him while carrying my lemon, without any inkling whatsoever on my end that those lemons I was regularly getting from the mini fridge were actually Dom Symeon's.

✢ ✢ ✢

Imagine how terribly embarrassed I felt when I learned this truth later on. I assumed the lemons in the mini fridge were the abbot's, when in fact his were always stored in the vegetable crisper of the big fridge at the back of the Refectory (and all the while Abbot Ed kept wondering why his stock never seemed to decrease). We were, of course, all laughing about the hilarious mix-up when we realized what was happening.

✢ ✢ ✢

At 7 A.M., I Zoomed with a former classmate from seminary during the '90s in Texas. Chris and I reconnected through Facebook several years ago after I moved to California and became an Episcopalian. I knew from Facebook that he had become an Anglican and later a rector at a parish in Texas. I was intrigued when I found out that Chris had converted to Catholicism not too long ago. Unable to contain my curiosity any longer, I initiated Zoom contact with him and got to hear his fascinating story. I thought to myself, "What a 'coincidence' that I'd connect with two Anglicans, one after another, who had both converted to Catholicism: first Jon Sweeney of Paraclete Press, and now Chris—while I was at the abbey and contemplating my own issues related to their shared experiences.

With my personal wonderings even more intensified, I had to ask myself what could possibly be behind these recent connections that only seemed to seize my attention at this time and in this place. Sensing our initial conversation to be just the beginning of something potentially deeper, Chris and I agreed to keep in touch.

✢ ✢ ✢

The spectacular sight of the cloud formations with their grayish shades accentuating the late afternoon sky put me in a somber mood. While pensively admiring the vast skies (to be sure, I've not seen anything like it in Los Angeles, not even close), I felt like the earth was mildly moving around me. I didn't make much of it until I observed something different happening to me while at Vespers.

Each time I stood up to bow down during the Gloria Patri, I felt like I was losing my bearings. I knew I had felt something similar before. It dawned on me that my first vertigo episode, some three years ago, might be recurring. My suspicion didn't seem far-fetched because I had no other way to explain the familiar experience. I naturally wished it would go away on its own, as it did before, and hopefully soon.

19 APRIL
sunday

Vertigo Spells

My vertigo-like feeling unfortunately didn't go away as I had hoped. During Lauds I realized that if I didn't hold on to the back seat of the pew in front of me while standing, I'd for sure lose my balance. The unstable feeling I was having became worse during Mass each time I would shift position from sitting to standing. I was beginning to feel miserable—to think it was Divine Mercy Sunday and I was clearly not sensing God's mercy for me that morning—despite Fr. Elias's upbeat delivery of his homily. In fact, I was secretly wishing for the Mass to end quickly so I could end my own agony, too.

I knew I would be fine so long as I maintained a stationary position, especially sitting. But if I stood for a period of time, I couldn't bear it unless I held on to something to keep my balance. In particular, abrupt movements put me off-kilter. Another unwelcome issue to deal with, I moaned inside—and why now?

When I brought up my predicament to Dom John Paul, he tried to be helpful by explaining my possible case scenario—using some foreign-sounding medical terms I had no clue about—and afterward prescribing some tablets for me to take, which I did, except nothing happened to alter my condition. Worse, I felt that nobody around me could relate to my quiet agony. Not that I wanted badly to call attention to myself, but I bet only those who have suffered from vertigo can commiserate with the awful feeling I was having. I also became increasingly self-conscious during communal prayers because of my awkwardness in trying to flow with the liturgical movements of standing, bowing, and sitting down. Utterly resigned to it, I just prayed (what else was left for me to do?)—hoping desperately that my vertigo episodes would simply end.

✢ ✢ ✢

At 9 A.M., Dom John Paul and I helped set up a Zoom meeting for the abbot's family so he could do a virtual Mass, especially for his mom, whom he had not seen since February. This was Abbot Ed's first Zoom experience saying Mass in front of my laptop, which rested on my table in the office. (We converted my office space into a mini church with an altar in the middle.) I could tell his mom was delighted to be able to connect, even via Zoom.

At 12:30 P.M., Abbot Ed conducted another Mass via Zoom, this time with a prominent family friend whose patriarch was celebrating his ninetieth birthday. The family members Zoomed in from different parts of the country and the world. It was a gratifying time for everyone, including the abbot, who counted the Zoom event as a special extension of his ministry to the friends of the abbey.

✢ ✢ ✢

Finding an outlet for my vertigo frustration that day, I got a kick out of assembling a collage of different photos I took of the chairs, tiles, bricks, steps, and posts around the abbey, and I posted it on Facebook with the caption "I have now counted them all"—referencing the serious task of doing so as the main culprit why I was suffering from some strange form of dizziness. For me, humoring myself was the least I could do to maintain my sanity! And believe it or not, it helped lift me out of my rut.

✢ ✢ ✢

God has some little ways of consoling a weary soul like me. On my way back to my office, after taking an afternoon snack at the Refectory (my supreme favorite cassava cake given to the monks by the Blue Sisters), whom should I bump into but Dom Symeon, smiling from ear to ear, carrying a plastic bag full of lemons—just for me! I wanted to hug him (but I didn't, as he might have been scandalized, not to mention the women in the office nearby who might catch sight of us from their open windows). It was so sweet of him to have gone out of his way to buy me those lemons.

20 APRIL
monday

My Own Cloister Walk

Time and again I get the itch to don my social butterfly garb—I love interacting with people, especially people I love—but at the same time, people in general, particularly crowds, wear me out fairly easily. I'm one of those borderline folks who score almost even on the Myers-Briggs introvert/extrovert scale. Because people always see the relational side of me, they readily conclude that I must be highly extroverted. In all honesty, I draw my energy from the inside. I often need my quiet space or else I feel depleted.

I declared today my own "hermit day," as I wanted to be alone for the most part. I lay in bed and rested my body for most of the morning. In the afternoon I engaged in my new contemplative hobby, *foto divina*. This time I decided to focus my picture-taking inside and around the monastic enclosure. To borrow the title of Kathleen Norris's book, I did my own contemplative "cloister walk" while capturing every nook and cranny inside the monastery.

Once you enter the mini door of the enclosure from the main chapel, and you pass the sacristy on the left and the aumbry (the room where the tabernacle is) on the right, you come to a covered patio. At the front is a small quadrangle with a nicely landscaped courtyard that Fr. Elias helped design (with some bonsai plants surrounding the center). An emblem of the Benedictine medal carved on stone, with water flowing gently through it, serves as the focal point. Two open corridors (left and right) bracket the quadrangle. On the opposite end is another passageway that leads to the monks' quarters, which are built like an inverted U. My room is located at the dead-end where the two corridors come together, with another courtyard in the middle. There wasn't anything extraordinary about the architectural design of the quarters, but the entire structure exudes a holy ambience that I can't fully explain. It's probably what the author Philip Sheldrake (my former professor at Notre Dame) refers to as "a sense of place and space," which evokes an unmistakable spiritual presence.

> *The entire structure exudes a holy ambience that I can't fully explain.*

I love being inside this monastic enclosure, and I never grow tired walking around it. In more ways than one, these tranquil surroundings serve as my place of refuge at the end of every day—a consecrated space, like my own private portal to God. Before retiring this evening, I posted some pictures on Facebook, giving everyone a little inside look at the cloister.

A peek inside the monastery enclosure

21 APRIL
tuesday

A Perfectly Good Day

When the abbot saw the Facebook postings of the cloister that I did the night before (yes, he faithfully checks his Facebook each day), his first remark initially caught me off guard: "Nobody has ever done this before!" I was ready to launch into my apology—thinking I must've violated some monastic protocol—when Abbot Ed continued by complimenting how beautifully I had captured the very serene atmosphere of the enclosure. Sigh!

From that moment on, even with the abbot's assurance that I wasn't crossing the line, I became a little more conscious about my movements around the abbey. Lest I forget, I am still officially a guest, even if nobody ever makes me feel like one. In fact, many times I find myself moving about like one of the monks—cleaning my own dishes and helping dry them, washing my clothes, tidying my room, freely partaking of their common food (even raiding the fridge once in a while for a late-night scoop of Pinoy ice cream). Being so completely welcomed has given me almost nothing to worry or complain about, even though I am stranded here.

✢ ✢ ✢

In need of a little physical stretching from my fast-becoming sedentary mode in my office, I finished up my day with an early evening stroll outside the abbey compound before night fell completely, signaling me to head back before my night blindness took over.

It was a perfectly good day!

22 APRIL
wednesday

Zoom and Doom

Life keeps moving for me—sometimes rapidly, as though there are no inhibiting factors—while I engage in my ongoing work with CenterQuest, albeit from a great distance. Our six-week eCourse on the Enneagram, in cooperation with the Arizona Enneagram Association, kicked off last Monday, and we're gearing up for our meet-and-greet Zoom for the new class. By now I have collected a bunch of eye-catching shots of the abbey that would make some great virtual backdrops for my Zoom screen. I want to showcase to everyone that, contrary to what some might imagine, I have actually landed in paradise!

I learned recently that the Henri Nouwen class I was supposed to teach at Vancouver School of Theology in July will now be converted to a full-blown Zoom class. There goes my much-anticipated trip to British Columbia this summer! I predict the same might happen to my weekend retreat at St. Benedict Center in Schuyler, Nebraska, also scheduled for mid-July. To my consolation, at least the two July events have not been cancelled altogether. Zoom has become a convenient fall back. At least I'll have the coolest abbey backdrops to display on my Zoom teaching engagements!

✢ ✢ ✢

BBC News ran a thought-provoking news article that I came across today with this headline: "Coronavirus: World Risks 'Biblical' Famine Due to Pandemic—UN." After skimming the content of the article, I had two immediate reactions: I was perturbed, and I felt guilty. The seriousness of our present situation and its global repercussions are coming into ever-sharper focus and commanding my attention. Sometimes I debate whether I'd be better off not reading the news anymore.

Although I seriously questioned whether a famine was conceivable in our day, I caught myself silently praying "Lord, have mercy," as I reckoned with the possibility of this prediction. By the same token, I experienced a momentary twinge of guilt as I assessed the relative abundance I continue to enjoy here in the abbey.

The image of all that leftover food on the meal table haunts me. For whatever it's worth, reading the news today brought me to my knees and drove me to implore God's mercy for all of humankind. Without a doubt, our new reality is a serious one with which we must reckon.

 The seriousness of our present situation and its global repercussions are coming into ever-sharper focus ...

23 APRIL
thursday

"Beingness"

My morning at my office began with an early Zoom meeting with our mentors at CenterQuest. During our preliminaries, I proudly clicked on my new abbey backdrops so I could boast to our team how blessed I was to be surrounded by beauty in this remote place—my own way of assuring them that I am perfectly OK where I am stranded.

Before we broke into two groups—I facilitated one group, while Nina Lau-Branson, our School of Spiritual Direction program assistant and mentors supervisor, led the other one—I had to forewarn everyone that if I abruptly disappeared from their screen, it simply meant there was a brownout in the abbey.

In SSD, we practice the format of group spiritual companioning introduced in our module on Group Spiritual Direction taught by Lisa Myers and facilitated by our mentors in meeting with their mentoring groups throughout the program. For the next hour and a half, after brief check-ins, we companioned one another using the Open Circle format for contemplative group spiritual companioning created by

Lisa that involves the group in prayerful preparing, presenting presence, listening presence, and several cycles of responding presence, as well as shared reflection on our experience. It was such a rich and refreshing time of reconnection—of communal presence and mutual support, which was precisely what my soul has been longing to receive and give. I came away from our Zoom time appreciative of how we have learned to engage group companioning and feeling spiritually full; I've truly missed all of our SSD mentors!

✧ ✧ ✧

Christine Valters Paintner is a colleague and friend of mine and a fellow Benedictine oblate. She is the online abbess at AbbeyoftheArts.com, a virtual "monastery without walls" that she manages from her current home in Galway, Ireland. Today Christine excerpted this paragraph from her recent book *Illuminating the Way: Embracing the Wisdom of Monks and Mystics* and posted it on Facebook:

> In monastic tradition, stability is another of the great virtues. On a literal level, stability was the vow the monks made to stay with one community their whole lives. This was to avoid the practice of going from one monastery to another, always leaving when conflict arose or dissatisfaction entered in. As the desert mothers and fathers knew, *you carry yourself wherever you go. So to leave a place to avoid certain dynamics or relationship patterns, you will only discover them again in the next place you arrive.* (emphasis mine)

She followed her own excerpt with this question, worthy of pondering: "What are the patterns and dynamics that you find constantly emerging in your relationships with other people?"

Having just addressed the topic of stability with the monks here at the start of Holy Week, I found this quote especially relevant—not just to monks in general, including the particular monks I presently live with—but to me personally. The last two sentences, which I've deliberately highlighted in italics, spoke to me directly because they remind me of the crucial importance of "beingness"—who we are at our deepest core: our true and unique self.

> *Centeredness ... remains the most solid foundation for any practice of stability.*

As I emphasized during my presentation to the monks on stability, centeredness (the first of the three Cs) remains the most solid foundation for any practice of stability. Either our grounding, or rootedness, is in God or it is in something else. Indeed, stability is foremost an issue of identity; either we live out of our true self in God or out of our false self—or more accurately, our manifold false selves. We always have the choice of which we will live out.

Since all of us are still far from perfect, the broken and flawed parts of us will always show forth in our relationships more than anywhere else. We will always be "under construction" as far as our relational deficits are concerned, so in the end it matters not whether we choose—or don't—to work at it; we carry who we are all the time, whenever and wherever we go. How I am in the United States with the people I circulate with there will be how I am in this abbey with the monks I live with in the present time. It's only a question of who I want and choose to be—which will determine the health or unhealthiness of my relational patterns.

It's very easy to put up a good front, or wear a mask, or choose to adapt, or assimilate in a new environment with new people around. But sooner or later I am bound to relate just as I've always related—always within the tensional reality of my own woundedness and healing. Thus I can be a wounded wounder or a wounded healer in my relationships, depending upon how and where I choose to operate from.

I am keenly aware that even though I'm not a monk, bound within the confines of a particular community, the expansive principle of stability still holds true—particularly inner stability, or what we call stability of the heart. Coming to the abbey, I am not oblivious of the fact that I also carry with me certain relational wounds based on where I come from, some still raw and unhealed. This recognition is crucial even as I enter into a new set of relationships in this new place.

In a number of his writings, Henri Nouwen referred to the trilogy of the false-self dynamics manifested in the erroneous belief that my identity rests on: what I do (performance), what I have (power), and what people say (popularity). The moment I succumb to operating out of any or all of these false identities, my relational dynamics with the people around me on a daily basis will inevitably be affected.

The expansive principle of stability still holds true— particularly inner stability "

After reading and reflecting upon Christine's piercing words today, I made a vow to free myself from any pressure to be someone other than who I truly am. I cannot afford to carry an additional internal burden when I am already wrestling with the external burdens brought on by this new reality.

This brief review of inner stability, roused by Christine's quote, is quite liberating as I move forward in this liminal space that God has opened up for me at this time and place.

✦ ✦ ✦

Today was also special in a different sort of way. Dom Carlo arranged for Loury to drive me to town so I could procure some much-needed personal supplies that I was slowly running out of, such as basic toiletries. This was my first time to emerge from the abbey after more than a month inside. With our certified clearance from the *barangay* (local town center) and our face masks ready, we proceeded to the nearby Gaisano Mall.

Everything appeared quite normal except for the mandatory face masks for everyone entering, temperature checks and hand sanitizer application at the door, and strict social distancing inside. Since I'm not much of a mall person, I went straight to Watsons for my preferred one-stop shopping. In less than twenty minutes I was done. On my way out, I thought about going inside the supermarket section in case I saw something I might need. Sure enough, I spotted a can of water-based Baygon spray to combat my insect enemies, and I grabbed a bag of Pinoy Clover Chips for my comfort-food snack. In line at the checkout counter I saw a small imported jar of Nutella spread that I thought Dom Pietro would appreciate, so I picked it up for him.

The first thing I did when we got back to the abbey was to spray my office with Baygon. I watched with vengeful delight as the mosquitoes dizzily fell to the ground, one by one. But my mission had just begun; taking the can with me to church, I liberally sprayed Baygon all around my seating area, right before

Vespers. It felt good, even though I was still having vertigo spells. I decided I would remain seated for most of the service so I wouldn't lose my balance.

At Compline that night, during the usual singing of *Regina Caeli*, when the monks move to the front pew and stand to face the statue of Our Lady of Montserrat, I noticed Dom Carlo covering his nose with his handkerchief. (Later I would learn that he was allergic to Baygon, so for his sake, I quit my vendetta against the mosquitoes at church and confined it to my office space.)

My "ora et **labada**" (laundry time) |

24 APRIL
friday

My Shorts Story

I t's Friday and it's laundry day for me again. For this second round, I thought I'd finally befriended the computerized washing machine, for it didn't give me anymore headaches. Everything went smoothly and I was a happy camper. To document my "triumphant" laundry session, I had Dom Jared take a picture of my contented face, and of course I posted it on Facebook.

I didn't bring many pants with me on this trip; I left most of them in Manila, along with my other belongings. I've just kept cycling through the few pairs I have with me. With all of them in the washer, I only had my shorts left to wear while waiting for my laundry to complete its cycle. After my laundry was done, it didn't occur to me to change out of my walking shorts; after all, the weather was a bit warm.

Without thinking anything of it, I went about participating in the usual liturgy throughout the day—Sext, Vespers, Compline—wearing my shorts with matching slippers, in typical California fashion. I was totally comfortable with my getup, but it never crossed my mind that others around me might not be—especially during the liturgy inside the church.

143

Nobody said anything to me except, one time, when I was casually complaining to the abbot about the unwanted presence of the mosquitoes in church, he teasingly remarked that the mosquitoes were probably too attracted to my exposed legs, hinting that it might help if I quit wearing shorts.

Later I recalled a monk at the Manila Abbey telling me gently but directly, last time I was there, to wear pants instead of shorts during liturgy and mealtimes. My impression was that this abbey was a little more informal, but maybe I stood out here because it's just them and me, particularly when they were all wearing their monk habits while I was in my walking shorts.

Whether it was kosher or not to wear shorts around the abbey, I never really knew for sure because I never got the chance to ask anyone. I just stopped wearing them at church or any time I was with the monks for meals at the Refectory.

Coffee, Tea, and TP

Today was my seventh Zoom meeting of the week and, boy, am I thankful I only have one left this morning—a spiritual direction session with someone from Pasadena, California, at 7:30 A.M. I generally enjoy Zooming with people, but this week has seemed like overkill. Or perhaps I am slowly getting weary of the new Zoom routine: because of the time zone difference between the US and the Philippines, my Zoom sessions are often back to back since I am working within a limited window of time.

✢ ✢ ✢

The gift shop happened to be open today, so I stopped in to buy some souvenir gifts for friends in Manila and the US—including a few bags of the abbey's famous Monks' Blend Premium Coffee, a combination of Arabica and Robusta beans produced at their nearby factory. I also got some St. Benedict bracelets and key chains, Monks' Roasted Peanuts, and some things for myself, including two boxes of locally produced Turmeric Instant Herbal Tea. Regularly drinking turmeric has always worked wonders for me, and I realized that I was out of my Zyflamend anti-inflammatory tablets. I was excited to try this local product that boasts of having ten essential healing ingredients, among them *Gynura procumens*, whatever that is! With the pandemic in mind, I am more than willing to try anything and everything that promises to keep me healthy and boost my immunity.

✦ ✦ ✦

As I was passing from my office through the corridor leading to the courtyard of the monastic enclosure on my way back to my room, I suddenly remembered I also was almost out of toilet paper. (My room was fully stocked when I first arrived in mid-March, which seemed like more than enough for the couple of weeks I would be at the abbey.) I made a brief stop at the guest toilet inside the Confession and Counseling Room, helped myself to an extra roll of toilet paper (I was a bit timid to ask any of the monks for it), and tucked it into my gift shop bag. I figured I could always say my confession to Fr. Elias later.

26 APRIL
sunday

Lasting Impressions

Today was an especially gorgeous day—bright and sunny, but not warm. The whole area looked and smelled fresh. As scheduled beforehand with the abbot, I staged a photo shoot of the monks after Mass, with everyone present, posing cooperatively in front of the altar. Two quick takes and we were done. I particularly requested this group shot to add as a climax to the slideshow I was putting together, featuring my choice collection of abbey photos.

Recently I have been obsessed with the idea of gathering all the iPhone pictures I have accumulated over the past month or so and converting them into a four to five-minute slideshow, complete with background music. I've lost count how many times I have rearranged the slide sequencing, added and deleted shots, changed the music score, and so on. This ongoing task has occupied my time, here and there, but I have been reveling in the creative process overall—a good outlet for my energy.

✦ ✦ ✦

At 10 A.M., we set up another Zoom Mass for the abbot's mother and the rest of the family, followed by an informal chat with the family members. Then at 1 P.M., Abbot Ed conducted a funeral Mass via Zoom for one of the oblates whose father just passed away. With all that the abbot had to attend to, he still made himself available to the family of this oblate, again as part of what he considered to be his ministry. After viewing the highly emotional service on Zoom (followed by the cremation ceremony), I was profoundly touched by the abbot's heart of compassion. Whether for a prominent family or an ordinary oblate, he makes time for those in need.

✤ ✤ ✤

On my way back to my room, I saw Fr. Elias approaching in my direction and I called for his attention. Grabbing the chance to clear my conscience, I owned up to stealing one of his extra rolls of toilet paper from the restroom of the Confession and Counseling Room. Either he didn't believe I was truly repentant or that I had really sinned against heaven; Fr. Elias simply shrugged off my lame confession and proceeded on with a puzzled smile.

✤ ✤ ✤

After our Vigils (in anticipation of the Feast of Our Lady of Montserrat tomorrow), I found a bag full of toilet paper hanging from the doorknob of my room when I returned from chapel. Thinking it too much, I planned on returning some to Fr. Elias the very next day.

27 APRIL
monday

Not-So-Good Awakening

Today is the feast day of Our Lady of Montserrat, a Marian title associated with the statue of the Virgin and Child, considered one of the only Black Madonna images in Europe and popularly referred to as *La Moreneta* (the little dark-skinned one). The original statue is venerated at the Benedictine Santa Maria de Montserrat Abbey in Catalonia, a thirty-minute drive from Barcelona. Santa Maria de Montserrat is the same abbey from which the first Benedictine monks, who arrived in the Philippines in 1895, originated. In fact, it was Abbot Sebastià Bardolet himself, the abbot of Montserrat at the time, who brought a replica of the original statue from Spain to the Philippines in 1997, and it remains enthroned in a glass case in the center of the Abbey of the Transfiguration church.

✧ ✧ ✧

As a young Catholic boy, I developed a special devotion to Mary, and I was fascinated with the famous apparitions of the Virgin in both Lourdes and Fatima. I even drew a sketch of both events when I was in elementary school. As with many other Catholic devotional pieties I engaged in while growing up, I later dismissed my allegiance to Mary, which I judged as excessive and bordering on Mariolatry.

When I became a Benedictine oblate, I was once again exposed to the practice of venerating Mary, but this time I experienced a marked shift in my perspective. This happened while I was at a Benedictine monastery in Pecos, New Mexico, around May 2007, during a series of celebrations in honor of Mary. The reverence accorded to Mary was deeply moving for me. I was impressed with how the Benedictine emphasis on Mary consistently and ultimately pointed to Christ, as evidenced by the lyrics of the several Marian hymns we sang. Once again, the Hail Mary and the Magnificat took on fresh meaning for me and I regained not just a healthy respect but a tremendous sense of awe for the unique role of Mary as *theotokos* (the God-bearer), which I had trivialized for such a long time.

I still may not subscribe to all the standard devotions directed to Mary, nor wholly embrace every doctrine associated with her that faithful Catholics hold, but I have honestly and significantly altered and expanded my otherwise narrow view of her. Over the years I have gradually resolved, in my heart, the major objections I once had to her. Today I can sing *Salve Regina* and *Regina Caeli* as legitimate hymns of praise to Mary without reservation.

On this special day commemorating Our Lady of Montserrat, I joined the community in honoring the Virgin Mary. As was customary, we ended the celebration by reciting together the *Memorare* (Remember, O Most Gracious Virgin Mary), an intercessory prayer directed to the Blessed Virgin taken from the last page of the abbey pamphlet entitled

"Devotion in Honor of Our Lady of Montserrat":

> *Remember, O most gracious Virgin Mary, that never was it known that anyone who fled to thy protection, implored thy help, or sought thy intercession was left unaided. Inspired with this confidence, I fly to thee, O Virgin of virgins, my Mother; to thee do I come; before thee I stand, sinful and sorrowful. O Mother of the Word Incarnate, despise not my petitions, but in thy mercy hear and answer me. Amen.*

Having affirmed my renewed devotion to Mary, I would lie if I didn't at least admit that every time we invoked this *Memorare* prayer, the first line always gave me pause, especially the phrase "never was it known that anyone who fled to thy protection, implored thy help, or sought thy intercession was left unaided."

✛ ✛ ✛

Since I left the States several months ago, my School of Spiritual Direction program codirector Lisa Myers and I have each been working intensively to upgrade our Group Spiritual Direction module in order to increase its duration from four to six weeks to provide more time for practical exercises. Lisa, who is the passionate instructor, has been pouring tremendous energy into preparing new ways to present the content she has created for this course in print and on video. I, on the other hand, have been supporting her on the technical side of things. After many long hours on the phone coordinating our efforts, we are officially ready to kick off the course next Monday. This is a major breakthrough for us, considering the intricate and tedious process involved in changing the Moodle format for the course and getting everything up to speed.

I personally have breathed a big sigh of relief, as I know Lisa is ready to carry the course forward on her own, now that all the changes to Moodle and technical groundwork have been laid. Now I can focus more on supervising the three other online courses we are about to run simultaneously: the Enneagram, Soul Companioning, and Spiritual Formation classes. I will be cofacilitating the latter with Val Dodge Reyna, one of CenterQuest's original founding members, who is based in Michigan. All these will take place while I am stationed in this remote abbey. Oh, the wonders of technology—the very boon and bane of our existence!

✤ ✤ ✤

Brownouts have been occurring a lot more frequently lately in the surrounding area, but they normally come and go—usually characterized by fairly short interruptions that you learn to cope with after a while. This morning I was in the middle of another important Zoom call to Singapore and without warning my screen froze; the next minute the internet signal was gone. Because all electrical connection went dead—this time, lasting for a couple of hours—I had no way of even texting the person I was on the call with to let him know why we were abruptly cut off.

Since there was nothing else to do, I retired to my room, where I spent a good while reading a copy of Abbot Ed's dissertation dealing with monasticism—a rich read as I was being initiated into its contemporary setting here in the abbey. Fully absorbed, I almost finished it in a single sitting.

As soon as the electricity came back on, around midafternoon, I reemerged from my room and headed back to my office. The first thing I did there was to text Zerah, the Singaporean guy I was on Zoom with in the morning, explaining why we had suddenly been cut off.

Thankfully, the brownout incident with Zoom has not reoccurred—at least not for an extended period of time. I still get cut off occasionally, while on the phone or on Zoom, but just for a few minutes. Over time, I have gotten used to these minor disruptions. I've been informed that as soon as the abbey can order the needed parts for the generator to fully function, things will operate like "normal" again. But with the lockdown, there is no way to procure the much-needed parts. Hearing the word *normal* gives me pause. I wonder when—or even if—normal will ever return.

✢ ✢ ✢

Toward the end of the afternoon, I found more unwelcome news in my email inbox: Cebu Pacific Air just cancelled my rebooked May 1 flight to Manila. Immediately I shot an email to Leeboy to try to rebook the flight to mid-May, if possible.

This time, with conscious resolve, I refused to dwell on this new development, and I went on with the rest of my work for the day with relative calmness of mind and heart. In the evening, after Vespers, we had the customary feast celebration during dinner at the Refectory. Aside from the special food served, we had ice cream for dessert. There's nothing like Pinoy ice cream when it comes to the tropical fruit flavors and other combinations I go for: mango, avocado, buko salad, ube-queso, or ube-macapuno. After battling the toothache on the left side of my mouth a couple of weeks ago, I have come to master the art of chewing on the right side. Since then I haven't had to deal with another agonizingly painful tooth episode.

Afterward, I went back to my office to attend to some high-priority work and ended up staying a little later than usual. Feeling stuffed from all the food I ate, I thought of trying out the turmeric herbal tea I recently purchased from the Abbey Gift Shop. So I headed back to the Refectory for hot water, then ran back to my room and quickly pulled out a sachet from the tea box. Imagining it as a way to cleanse my system, I squeezed lemon into my hot tea and even added a teaspoon of apple cider vinegar. Whether true or not, at least it felt like the tea slowly washed away the richness of all the food I consumed this evening.

In retrospect, maybe it didn't. Maybe it was all in my mind, because just past midnight I woke up from a horrible nightmare, screaming at the top of my lungs without knowing why. Realizing what had just happened, I wondered with concern whether I had disturbed the monks on either side of my room (Fr. Elias on my right and Dom Carlo on my left).

After I quieted down, I tried to get back to sleep, but to no avail. Turning on the small lamp on my bedside table, I sat up and reached out for Mark Nepo's *The Book of Awakening* (what an apt title!) and read until my eyes grew tired and I gradually fell back to sleep.

28 APRIL
tuesday

My Field of Dreams

I woke up around 4 A.M., still clutching Mark Nepo's *The Book of Awakening*. While trying to summon up what I had dreamed about, I geared myself up for Lauds. (I usually needed at least forty-five minutes to attend to my morning routine.)

The first chance I saw Dom Carlo, before I took my breakfast, I curiously asked him if he heard my screaming the night before. Shaking his head, he assured me he was in his own dreamland, unaware of any external noise. Fr. Elias had a similar response when, upon returning the bag of toilet paper to him, I asked him the same thing. He added that it wouldn't surprise him if none of the other monks heard anything either since most of them fall sound asleep as soon as they go to bed. These assurances put to rest my worry that I had created a disturbance in the very quiet enclosure.

✤ ✤ ✤

When I went back to my room, after a quick bite for breakfast, another bag full of toilet paper rolls was waiting for me on my front door. Then I remembered mentioning to Dom Symeon, in passing, that I had run out. Blown away by Fr. Elias's and now Dom Symeon's responsiveness to my needs, I can hardly believe that they've both gone out of their way to ensure I am well taken care of during my stay in the abbey.

As for Dom Symeon, either he is extremely sensitive to my minutest concerns or he is simply taking his role as assistant cellarer of the abbey responsibly! I suppose one of the reasons I often see Dom Symeon at the administration building coordinating with the women in the office is that cellarers and subcellarers are responsible for running the physical plant of the monastery, acting as stewards of its foodstuff and other supplies.

✧ ✧ ✧

After the Zoom webinar for our Enneagram class, which I sat in on for about an hour and a half, I went back to my desk work for the morning, reviewing first my to-do list for the day, as was my habit. I became distracted by a loud text alert on my iPhone. The minute I picked it up, I got further distracted when I accidentally clicked on my camera icon. Before long, I was thumbing through the series of photos I'd taken over the last five days. I was riveted by two particular shots I forgot I had taken when I left the abbey with Loury on April 23.

I recalled asking Loury to stop the van so I could capture the captivating scenery as we passed through the green fields on our way out toward the highway. The incredible visual impact was not something I anticipated when I reviewed the two shots later on, so much so that I could hardly wait to post them on Facebook. The caption I gave to the post was "The Monastery Field of Dreams"—a bit ironic given the nightmare that was still haunting me.

Within seconds I saw the abbot "like" my post and reply with these words: "A very moving photo. A symbol of hope and fruitfulness with rice grains budding forth." Another person followed suit and posted something similar: "Beautiful! Promise of plentiful harvest as well as a future full of hope."

Overwhelmed, I took a short, contemplative pause, then began a mini *visio divina* (visual meditation exercise), gazing intently on my "field of dreams" while imagining the color of hope floating through my mind's eye. Instead of allowing my thoughts to fix upon my nightmare, I consciously refocused my inner energy toward the more life-giving notion of hope, visualizing its shape and texture against my present reality.

| The monastery "field of dreams"

| Open doors

29 APRIL
wednesday

Doors, Open Doors

I had another impulse—hoping it was a divine one—to take more pictures around the Abbey Church. And that's basically how I spent the large part of my morning, inside the chapel, creatively composing each and every shot in my mind before actually taking them.

The square-looking church is actually surrounded by transparent glass walls with a total of twenty-eight "open doors," seven on each side. I positioned myself in front of each door and photographed each of the twenty-eight doors from the inside out—with the focal point directed toward what you see outside each door, with the steel door frame itself framing each shot. When I reflected on the end result of my photo shoot, I was astounded when I realized how many different pieces of reality we can easily overlook when we fail to view things from various angles. When I posted this collection into a single composite photo

> **I realized how many different pieces of reality we can easily overlook when we fail to view things from various angles.**

on Facebook, I titled it "Doors, Open Doors," taken from one of the songs from the musical *The Lion, the Witch, and the Wardrobe*, inspired by C. S. Lewis's *The Chronicles of Narnia* and staged locally in the Philippines by Trumpets, the same theater group that recently performed the reimagined version of *Joseph the Dreamer*, which I saw in Manila before flying to Mindanao.

I breathed a prayer to myself, ending my post with the following words: "May God open the doors for us and may we see the beauty outside every door before us!"

Amen!

Outside view from one of the open doors |

Everything Benedictine

It's unbelievable to think that we've come to the end of another month. It seems to have flown by so swiftly. I don't know what got into me this time, but I had the idea of starting a new group page on Facebook for Benedictine spirituality lovers. Blame it on the fact that I've been breathing the Benedictine air around me, addressing Benedictine core values during my interaction with the monks last Holy Week, getting more deeply immersed in the Benedictine liturgy both day and night, and yes, attempting to live out the Benedictine spirit right here where I am. I figure I might as well be consistent and find a creative way to keep promoting the Benedictine way within and outside my own circle.

I've titled our group page "Benedictine Friends," with the subtitle "And anyone interested in everything Benedictine," so it doesn't come across as too exclusive. I spent most of the day designing the banner and drafting a simple "Rules of Engagement" document that potential members can adhere to easily. I don't have anything ambitious in mind, just hosting a relatively manageable-sized group to interact around a common interest.

Surrender

May 1-26

"If we are willing to persevere
through the depths of
struggle we can emerge
with ... surrender ... that takes us
beyond pain to understanding."

- JOAN CHITTISTER

1
MAY
friday

Benedictine Momentum

Today marks my thirty-fifth wedding anniversary. Two other events in May are special to our family: Mother's Day and Juliet's birthday. I've already resigned myself to missing our anniversary and Mother's Day, for it doesn't seem at all likely that I'll be home by then. However, I hope to make it back before May 18, my wife's birthday (assuming my May 16 flight doesn't get cancelled again).

✣ ✣ ✣

I officially launched our Benedictine Friends Facebook group page today and started issuing invitations to my immediate circle of close friends who are either oblates or friends of oblates and open and embracing of Benedictine values. Responses started to trickle in but at a certain point, I reached my limit on invitations, according to Facebook, to my utter disappointment.

As the end of the day approached, we had over twenty-five new members. The numbers dramatically increased before the close of the evening after Abbot Ed started inviting his own abbey contacts, who in turn invited others. The last I checked before calling it a night, our membership had swelled to more than a hundred. I was only hoping for about fifty to a hundred serious folks to come on board but, from the trend, it's evident many are eager to join in and be counted.

Rules of Engagement

Countless alerts inundated my Facebook page, notifying me that our Benedictine Friends page has reached over five hundred members. "Now what have I gotten myself into?" I asked myself, almost in disbelief. As I waded through the slew of posts, it became abundantly clear to me that posting the Rules of Engagement was now warranted, before things get unruly. This is the initial abridged version that I quickly posted at the top of the page; I omitted my elaborated commentary on each point:

1. We aim to **uphold** and **promote** (and hopefully live out increasingly) **Benedictine spirituality**.
2. We aim to be **ecumenical**.
3. We aim to be **global** and **international**.
4. We aim to exercise **generous hospitality** among us.
5. We aim to **celebrate diversity** of expression and involvement.
6. Lastly (at least for now!), we aim to be an **encouragement** to one and all through this page—"*that in all things God may be glorified,*" so keep this aim in mind if and when we engage in the forum or post anything.

Despite my few attempts to keep moving these rules to the top of the page, it is obvious that many are overlooking them, as evidenced by some of the postings, which I was tempted to delete straightaway (although I restrained myself from doing so). This has prompted me to post an addendum, to get the members' attention and clarify the rationale for our group's existence; I've requested that every new member read the rules and the addendum before posting anything on our timeline, which I hope will help filter out the "deletable" posts starting to clutter our feed.

※ ※ ※

Most of my dealings with Dom Carlo have been around business related to his multiple responsibilities in the abbey, especially his roles as guest master and personal secretary to the abbot. This evening, when he joined me for dinner, I witnessed another side of Dom Carlo that I never expected to have personal access to. He was in a chatty mood and freely shared bits and pieces of his own monastery escapades over the years, underscoring in particular a period in his life that was quite challenging for him. Hearing Dom Carlo transparently divulge these highlights, as well as some "lowlights," of his long monastic career, I felt privileged to be invited to experience a part of him I never would've known, were it not for his willing self-revelation.

Behind all the roles he plays at the abbey and the persona of confident strength he always projects, I saw for the first time a very vulnerable Dom Carlo. I felt his tender heart and his solid commitment to his vocation as he continues to wrestle with the ongoing demands of the monastic call to which he has given his life. I count it a privilege to know Dom Carlo as deeply as he wants to be known.

3 | MAY
Sunday

My Self-Inflicted Drama

I woke up in the wee hours past midnight, and when I tried to put myself back to sleep, my mind began fostering all kinds of thoughts—mostly things I needed to attend to. Lest I forget them, I typed them up on the Notes app on my iPhone, to be reminded later. By the time I'd covered everything, it was time to get up and go about my early morning ritual. It was already 4 A.M.

For the first time in a long time I felt sluggish, devoid of any motivation to attend Lauds in the next hour. Since I was already wide awake—and much earlier than usual—I stopped by my office at the administration building and worked on my laptop until the bell rang for Lauds. Something seemed a little off, but I couldn't figure out exactly what it was, except I found myself dillydallying on my way to the chapel. I've always loved the Divine Office and looked forward to participating in it, but today was a definite exception.

The morning liturgy didn't begin well for me. By this time, I should've memorized the whole drill, but I still found myself at a loss a couple of times in terms of where we were in the Lauds sequence, fumbling through the three different sets of liturgy materials I was holding in my hand. Thanks to Dom Jared who spotted my confusion and subtly called my attention to which booklet we were on (while I murmured inside why we had to keep switching booklets here and there). To be sure, the monks knew precisely which booklet to use, and when, like the back of their hands, and I was also supposed to by now. But I didn't, so I felt totally inept.

Not only was I not very present this early Sunday morning, but I was also impatient and critical in my spirit. I wondered whether the monks were just going through the motions—I mean, don't they get tired of the same liturgy and singing the same hymns over and over again? How many Alleluias, Our Fathers, and Glory Be's do we have to repeat before we're all prayed out? (Even my favorite Benedictus for Lauds and Magnificat for Vespers could become tiresome.)

For a split second I was shocked that I was thinking such things. While my mind could easily cough up some no-brainer responses to my own questions, it didn't negate the fact that my feelings were running contrary to any sound reason. At that point, nothing seemed to make sense. "Why am I feeling so rotten inside?" I wondered. It didn't help that my dizziness had not subsided. I actually began to question why my dizzy spells only occurred during liturgy—was I being "oppressed"?

Despite the strange struggle I was experiencing deep inside, I still managed to maintain my pious facade. None of the monks, I supposed, would've guessed anything about my foul Sunday mood. And I wasn't about to give myself away. I even assisted the abbot with his Sunday Zoom with his mother and family, and the whole proceeding went smoothly.

I spent the rest of the morning in my office as though it were an ordinary workday. The melancholic feel of the afternoon weather seemed to commiserate with my bad day, with the gloomy skies soon giving way to pouring rain. I took a photograph of the rain through my window and posted it on Facebook with a caption declaring my intention: "It's raining, it's pouring, and I am sleeping!" And sleep I did, like a log throughout the afternoon, until Vespers.

I made it through the evening liturgy without losing my balance—although I was still having dizzy spells—and afterward went straight to my room, skipping dinner as usual, to reflect on my lousy day. Like a deprived child unloading piled-up resentments on his parents, I recited my litany of complaints to God for failing to come through for me—that is, for not being quick to iron out my time-sensitive (read urgent) concerns, such as my going home soon.

Question after question, I pressed my charges against God with a demanding spirit. At the same time, I realized that my basic grievance had more to do with God not cooperating with my set agenda. I was audacious enough to demand why not!

Suddenly, as though God was catering to my self-inflicted drama, I remembered a couple of lines from my favorite C. S. Lewis book, *Till We Have Faces*—the climactic words of Queen Orual, the Greek mythological protagonist: "I know now, Lord, why you utter no answer. You are yourself the answer. Before your face questions die away. What other answer would suffice?" And just like that, I fell into silence, humbled and ashamed. It was cathartic!

The long corridor inside the cloister |

4

"If These Halls Could Speak"

To label today simply as a frenetically busy day would be imprecise. It's my manic Monday! Today we launched three of our eCourses with CenterQuest: our Group Spiritual Direction six-week module for our cohort 4 that Lisa, Nina, and I have been working hard on ever since I left the US in January; our Soul Companioning four-week class (cofacilitated by three of our CenterQuest folks originating from three different locations: Craig from Southern California; Vanessa from Victoria, British Columbia; and Margie from Oregon) with twenty-five students from the States, Canada, Indonesia, Singapore, India, Hong Kong, and the Philippines—representing six different time zones; and our Spiritual Formation class (through our Lifelong Learning Community [LLC] site), which I will be cofacilitating with Val from Michigan.

Last week we also began another six-week course on the Enneagram (also under our LLC) facilitated by Jaye Andres, executive director of the Arizona Enneagram Association. To top it off, my twelve-week online class on the spirituality of Henri Nouwen at Tyndale Seminary in Toronto, Canada, is rolling out simultaneously with all our CenterQuest May course offerings. An insane way to start the week, I know, but I am crazy excited!

Anticipating a jampacked Monday, I had planned on starting my day by taking a brisk walk with Dom Jared. Lately I have been catching sight of him through my office window on his early morning walk. Just the other day, I ran into Dom Myron returning from his walking exercise. The abbot himself, upon the advice of his doctor, has been regularly taking some short walks around the abbey. Obviously I got the wrong impression that only Dom John Paul, who looks quite fit, is committed to consistent physical exercise. I often see him in jogging pants, attending to his fitness routine. To my surprise, I've even witnessed him lifting weights in one of the vacant rooms late at night. Seeing the monks do their exercise is sufficient motivation for me to go back to my neglected walking practice and de-stress myself in the process.

Dom Jared and I went back to the new retreat center that Dom Paco showed me before; we climbed up the hill to the old monastery, back down, and toward the road opening up to the highway. Just to work up a sweat was gratifying enough for me, not to mention the chance to take more pictures of the inviting scenes along the way. Perhaps I have become so preoccupied with my own issues that I completely brushed aside the idea of exercising for my own good. I was glad I did so today, in this wonderful, vast place.

✢ ✢ ✢

Walking through the long orridors inside the cloister on my way back to my room to shower, it occurred to me that I must've passed through these halls countless times by now. I took a snapshot of a particular angle I really liked and posted it on Facebook with the following caption: "If these halls could speak." And really, I wondered inside what they might have to say—these quiet witnesses to my personal monastic escapades.

"If these halls could speak"

Right after posting my photo, I came upon a quote by *New York Times* bestselling author and pastor of *Life.Church* Craig Groeschel: "What feels like our worst interruptions may actually be God's greatest invitations" (posted by Christian musician/artist *TobyMac* on his Facebook blog). I could only exclaim a triple "**yes**" to it. Considering for a second what might be God's specific invitations for me spurred me to take the time to really explore them, to be able to name them one by one, and by God's enabling, to respond to them.

✣ ✣ ✣

The rest of the day I stayed practically glued to my desk, attending to the various demands of our online courses (the first day of classes always presents many expected and unexpected challenges, including technological glitches). It's not an exaggeration to say that my hands (especially my right one) felt numb from typing by the end of the day.

But here's the totally unanticipated part of my so-called manic Monday. While attending Vespers this evening, I noticed something different, to my huge relief. After my bouts of vertigo for the past couple of weeks, I felt normal for the first time—a whopping gift to receive at the end of my super demanding day. I'd like to think that my morning routine of freshly squeezed lemon in warm water with apple cider vinegar, plus turmeric-ginger tea with lemon in the evening, must have helped bring balance to my system! Or maybe my morning exercise made a difference. Whatever it was, my heart was overflowing with thankfulness to God!

✧ ✧ ✧

Before heading back to my room, I pulled aside Fr. Elias, who seemed to me uncharacteristically dispirited today. Actually, Dom Joaquin tipped me off earlier that Fr. Elias discovered one of his prized bonsai trees was missing from the courtyard, much to his dismay. Knowing how much this must have affected him, I wanted to hear out his sentiments and hopefully console him. Fr. Elias suspected that an outsider must have stolen it in broad daylight while the monks were resting during the early part of the afternoon. While assuring me he was OK, I could feel and understand his sense of loss. My heart goes out to him, especially since I have acquired a special liking for these lovely bonsai trees.

5 MAY
tuesday

Cooling Tactics

I was confronted with the local news today—about the government shutdown of ABS-CBN (a Philippine commercial television and new media network), which many deemed politically motivated. This breaking news—though not surprising given the controversial debates surrounding its franchise renewal—nearly ruined my mood for the entire day. On impulse, and against my better judgment, I shared my reactive sentiments—where else but on Facebook. This elicited a few counterposts. As much as I can help it, I avoid engaging in partisan political issues, keeping in mind that I have friends in opposing political camps. Carried away by my reaction, I even issued a challenge to anyone who disagreed with my position to freely "unfriend" me on Facebook, and I think a few took me up on it because I noticed soon after that the number of my Facebook friends decreased a bit.

✢ ✢ ✢

During the early afternoon I decided to spend an extended time at the Abbey Confession and Counseling Room, a cool place to hang out in more ways than one! The comfortable twin rooms are separated by a movable divider and tastefully decorated by Fr. Elias—and they have air conditioning! Earlier today I moved the standing fan from my room into my office, but as expected, it just kept blowing hot air around until I couldn't stand it anymore and I remembered this heavenly place, where I could cool off my hot head and my body.

On such warm days I fantasize about anything cold, such as the Vita Coco drink. I recalled seeing Dom Symeon munching on an ice candy the other day, so I opted to go to the Refectory and check out the merienda. When I saw it was the usual bread, I raided the freezer for some leftover ice cream. Lo and behold, there was a bunch of frozen avocado ice candies, so I sampled one. It was so creamy and tasty that I wondered why nobody was eating them except Dom Symeon. (I would revisit the freezer over the next couple of days.)

I asked Dom Symeon where these ice candies came from and learned that they were given to the monks by a group of nuns called the "Green Sisters." How lucky are these monks to have the Blue Sisters and the Green Sisters supply them with all these goodies! I remember noticing a couple of sisters at Lauds and Mass wearing dark-green habits. I learned that these Green Sisters are from a local congregation called the Sisters of the Rural Mission Order of St. Benedict, founded by a certain bishop from Bacolod Diocese in 1973. Officially, their congregation is not yet affiliated with the Benedictine family, although they conduct their vocation in the spirit of St. Benedict and his Rule.

One time I saw Dom Symeon carrying a bunch of Monks' Roasted Peanuts from the Abbey Gift Shop to the Green Sisters, whose house is located close to the western boundary of the abbey property. Roasted peanuts in exchange for ice candies? Mmmmm! As for me, I'll take ice candies over roasted peanuts any day!

✢ ✢ ✢

Because of the social distancing protocol, I never did get a chance to talk to any of the Green Sisters while I was in the abbey; I only saw them briefly from a distance during the morning liturgy. I wish I could have thanked them personally for the tasty ice candies I so enjoyed.

The wide-open skies of Malaybalay, Bukidnon |

6 MAY
wednesday

Blessed Sanctuary

On a warm sunny morning like this, I never tire of watching the vast, wide-open skies of Bukidnon from my office window, reminding me of the simple truth that God is the great Creator of earth and sky! Just the plain sight of God's glorious creation never fails to stir a sense of wonderment in me. Today, I feel this genuine sense of delight in God for spoiling me with such visual nourishment, calming my sometimes-restless soul. I don't dare be ungrateful for the unique state of blessedness I constantly enjoy in this equally blessed sanctuary.

> *Just the plain sight of God's glorious creation never fails to stir up a sense of wonderment in me.*

✢ ✢ ✢

Our Benedictine Friends group page has already ballooned to almost a thousand. Since I already almost completed my two versions of the abbey slideshow, I considered premiering them on the site by hosting a Facebook watch party—just as I've been seeing others do. I've never done a watch party before, so I did a little googling on how to go about it before finally settling on a date to stage it.

To create some anticipation, I immediately posted a "save the date" message for Saturday, May 9, at 10 A.M. I was so excited about the prospect of doing this for the first time, and I spent a lot of energy preparing for the event. For the nth time, I revised and upgraded the slide video, wanting so much to perfect it for our premiere.

Halo-Halo Delight

The moment I woke up I texted Abbot Ed, knowing he would already be awake, and greeted him with a "Happy Birthday." Today is the abbot's seventy-third birthday and, in the spirit of the Benedictine *ora eat labora*, I anticipated a sumptuous dinner celebration. (I was already imagining the dessert for the evening!)

Bringing my breakfast bowl to my office at 6:30 A.M., I launched into preparing for my back-to-back Zoom meetings, both meet-and-greet sessions with the participants of our CenterQuest Lifelong Learning Community (LLC) Spiritual Formation class at 7 A.M. and the CenterQuest School of Spiritual Direction (SSD) Soul Companioning class at 8:15. I was keyed up to share the PowerPoint presentation that I had prepared with the help of my Singapore contacts, Zerah and Lydia. (Lydia is an Indonesian graphic artist based in Singapore, who is also a participant in the Spiritual Formation class, as is Zerah.)

The short piece I am presenting is entitled "Overview of Our Spiritual Foundations." It synthesizes the basic interrelationship between spirituality and the constructs of spiritual formation, spiritual disciplines, spiritual companioning, spiritual community, and spiritual journey using the graphic symbol of the wagon wheel (which is also our CenterQuest logo, inspired by Henri Nouwen's concept of the hub, or the center, to which all the spokes are attached). It was through a casual chat with Zerah, early on, that the overview concept was "accidentally" germinated, and I was very pleased with our finished product, which we've been fine-tuning for several days. Today was our premiere presentation's "field test." After running the Soul Companioning class for thirty cycles already, this was the first time we've offered participants a detailed visual overview to help them better understand how the fields of spiritual accompaniment and spiritual formation fit within the broader realm of our spirituality and our spiritual journey.

I hosted both Zoom sessions, so as soon as the first one was done, I had to jump into the other class immediately. I was apprehensive about a potential brownout (which fortunately did not occur), but everything flowed well, and we garnered some positive reviews of the presentation.

After lunch, which I shared with Abbot Ed at the guest house, we were greeted outside by Rod and Tess Llacer, who brought with them two roasted *lechon* (roasted pig) and other dishes for the abbot's birthday celebration. Indeed, the food served at dinner was delectable. I'm not a lechon eater, so I didn't touch it, but I loved the oyster delicacy—so yummy! But the highlight of the celebration for me—and I suspect for everyone else, including the abbot—was the ultra-creamy *halo-halo* dessert (literally "mix-mix"—a blended concoction of sweet delicacies such as sweet beans, banana, and jackfruit, with a scoop of ice cream, ube, and leche flan on top of shaved ice), specially ordered from Kuya J Restaurant (whose grand opening took place on the same day last year, with three monk-priests in attendance and presiding in the eucharistic celebration). Kuya J has become rather popular because of its prime endorser, the well-known Philippine actor Jericho Rosales (whom many wrongly mistake for the owner). I had never before tasted anything like this version of halo-halo. (I wished there would be another opportunity to taste one again before I had to leave the abbey!)

Morning has broken

8 MAY
friday

Morning Has Broken

Midway through Lauds this morning, I couldn't resist gazing at the sky outside, where I could see the morning dramatically breaking right before my eyes, in all its glorious splendor. Mesmerized, I slowly inched my way out of the chapel while everyone was reciting the Gloria Patri with their heads bowed, hoping nobody would notice me. After capturing the enchanting scene with my iPhone camera, I cautiously snuck back inside, only to catch the abbot looking in my direction.

Feeling exposed, I later offered my apology to Abbot Ed for possibly distracting others during the liturgy. His response was gracious: "Well, what you did was simply a part of the worship experience." Abbot Ed was more than delighted by the series of photos I posted on Facebook afterward, which I titled: "Morning was breaking" and "Morning has Broken" (reminiscent of the popular song of the same title sung by Cat Stevens).

✢ ✢ ✢

For the third time, I engaged in *ora et labada* (laundry time). By now I am an expert in the laundry department. I have learned the art of carefully stretching my T-shirts and pants before and after putting them in the dryer, and smoothing them out by hand so I don't have to iron them. Except for a few polo shirts that are too crumpled, I settle for unironed clothes, for the most part (although I did ask Dom Carlo to have the "ironing lady" at the guest house press a few of my Sunday shirts a couple of times). In the back of my mind, I am hoping this might be the last time I will have to do all this—hoping against hope that I will fly back to Manila and then to Los Angeles in the next week or so.

At 10:30 A.M., I went back to my office to Zoom with Juliet and my two sons, Jonathan and David (along with Christy, David's fiancée). This was our first time connecting via Zoom as a family and I couldn't wait to share with them the final version of my "Dear Abbey" slideshow that I will premiere at Saturday's watch party for our Benedictine Friends members. Everyone absolutely loved it. It was great catching up and reassuring my family that I am in a good place, so there is no cause for their concern. At the same time, I requested a prayer that I might get a flight back to Manila soon and arrive in Los Angeles before Juliet's birthday on May 18.

9 MAY
saturday

Watch Party Snafu

The time came for the much-awaited watch party event. A little before 10 A.M., I cued up the two versions of my "Dear Abbey" slide video, with two other slideshows before it (featuring my Benedictine pilgrimage highlights from last year's trip to Germany, Austria, and Switzerland) as my preliminary showing (the "opening act" before the main feature). While doing so, I started issuing invitations to our members, reminding them of the event, which had just started. Abbot Ed was in the adjacent room in the administration building, also inviting others to join in.

While I could see the first slideshow on my laptop, Abbot Ed called my attention to the fact that it wasn't registering on his. Then, one after another, I began receiving texts from Dom Carlo and many others, informing me that they weren't seeing anything at all on their screens.

Nearly panicking, I tried everything I could think of to remedy the glitch, but to no avail; I hadn't the foggiest idea what was wrong. Meanwhile, my Facebook feed was flooding with comments, all saying the same thing—that their screen was blank.

By the time the second pilgrimage video popped up, the people who had signed up to watch were relieved to see the slides playing smoothly. I thought everything would work fine from then on. To my horror, when the main feature was supposed to come on, we had the same issue, which upset me no end. I felt very helpless as to what to do next, while folks were waiting to see the "Dear Abbey" video that I had so drummed up beforehand. It seemed like a lost cause. Utterly frustrated because of the disastrous outcome, all I could do was apologize to everyone.

Instead of continuing with the live showing, I resorted to posting the actual video on the site so people could watch it on their own. Seeing what I had just done, Weng, the techie family friend of the abbot's, came to my rescue and started his own watch party using the video I'd just posted, and it worked well. Although from my anxious perspective the whole event was a disaster, I was amazed that not a single soul complained; they just waited patiently. In an effort to compensate for the interruptions, I posted several different versions of my videos with accompanying words of apology. Needless to say, I needed time to recover from the stress of this morning's snafu, so I retired to my room to unwind a bit.

✦ ✦ ✦

Mildly traumatized—and soberly humbled—by the watch party event, where it seemed like Murphy's Law completely took over, I switched gears and started to attend to the different CenterQuest eCourses we are running. In the middle of trying to tie up some loose ends for one of our online classes, my oldest son, Jonathan, texted me—a rare occurrence. It soon became apparent that he wanted to unload something, so I paused what I was working on to respond to his texts, which kept on coming. I soon realized that it was a big deal for him to find in me an outlet for his frustrations. This was the most brutally honest and transparent chat I have ever had with my son—and one of the longest, all via text message. Who would've thought?

Although at certain points in our text conversation we were mildly arguing, and he was undoubtedly assuming a contrarian role for the most part, the whole exchange was refreshingly open, and Jonathan even thanked me at the end—especially when I genuinely affirmed the goodness of his heart— which was a relief. I could count on these types of conversations with David, my youngest, but this was a first with Jonathan, and I counted it a privilege to experience this long-distance connection with him. I still carried inside of me a certain amount of guilt and regret for being an absentee dad while he was growing up (unlike David, with whom I was more present, having come to my senses by then). Although I had addressed this issue with Jonathan when he graduated from high school (he's now thirty-two), it was reassuring to share this meaningful time with him today.

✢ ✢ ✢

Toward the latter part of the afternoon, I made a concerted effort to rebook my Philippine Airlines flight to Los Angeles for May 19 (the only available date and a day after Juliet's birthday). After a few maddening attempts, I was successful, albeit at an awfully steep cost of more than double my original round-trip ticket. As I shelled out the money for my one-way return flight, I felt regret for not seriously considering the possibility of taking a "sweeper flight" to Los Angeles the first time it was offered to stranded US citizens as well as green-card holders like me. Crossing my fingers that my local Cebu Pacific Air flight to Manila (already rebooked for May 16) would depart as scheduled, I could only hope and pray that I would finally make it home to the States.

Because of all this, I ended up missing Vespers. But I was somewhat consoled that I was able to make the reservation, despite the tedious process. When I told the abbot about my new plan, he seemed to sense my restrained excitement, as well as my lingering anxiety, and he reminded me to take things a step at a time and focus on ensuring that I got to Manila first (which of course makes sense).

10 MAY
sunday

Mother's Day Rains

First thing in the morning, I posted on Facebook a Mother's Day greeting from the abbey featuring a close-up shot of one of Fr. Elias's bonsai beauties. Midmorning, we staged a special Mother's Day Mass on Zoom with the abbot's family. Being a "mama's boy" growing up, I suddenly missed my own *nanay* (mother) while witnessing the abbot and his elderly mom connect through the screen affectionately (it's obvious they've been missing each other for quite a while now).

✦ ✦ ✦

The rainy season has definitely begun. Another heavy downpour came this afternoon, pounding on every corner of the monastery enclosure, with accompanying thunder and lightning. From the various parts of the enclosure's hallways, I observed the rain, taking pictures and occasionally being jolted out of my concentration by the flashes of lightning and booms of thunder. After the heavy rain subsided, I walked outside to capture the after-the-rain mood of the abbey surroundings and, of course, posted this series of photos on Facebook.

193

The Abbey Confession and Counseling Room

11 MAY
monday

Rainy Days and Mondays

After Terce this morning, we all gathered at the Abbey Confession and Counseling Room for my "live" showing of the two versions of my "Dear Abbey" slideshow video, which we attempted to premiere last Saturday through our Benedictine Friends group page. Abbot Ed and I decided to show the videos to the community before I leave the abbey. Dom Pietro made sure that the slide projector and screen were set up and ready the night before. We had to open up the movable divider separating the twin rooms to comfortably accommodate all the monks; all but one attended the showing.

This gathering was my chance to personally express my gratitude to the community for the warm hospitality they had extended to me throughout my stay in the abbey. And the video slideshow I had put together served as my special souvenir gift to them—the collected memories of my unforgettable stay in the abbey. As I was delivering my little gratitude spiel after the show—which everyone seemed to appreciate—I had to restrain myself from getting too emotional, even as I looked into each one of the faces of these monks, whom I've had the rare chance of getting to know and who have already, in one way or another, become a part of me.

The one monk who went out of his way to approach me afterward was Dom Myron, the abbey organist who regularly accompanies the monks in singing Matins, Lauds, Vespers, and the daily Mass. The sensitive musical artist in him showed itself in the way he thanked me and commented in great detail on my choice of background music for the video: the lyrics, the tempo, the mood it evoked, even its synchronous timing with certain slide themes. That meant a lot to me since Dom Myron seems to be a very private person who seldom speaks and always keeps to himself. In fact, he is the monk I've interacted with the least.

Though he has consistently maintained a quiet demeanor, I discovered a curious side to him once when, catching me totally by surprise, he asked me something about one of my sons. I was mildly flattered when he admitted that he had googled me. "At least Dom Myron was interested enough to know more about my background," I thought.

There's no question Dom Myron is a talented and dedicated musician who not only has composed music for the Men's Choir to sing during Mass but has also taken it upon himself to keep upgrading the abbey's Divine Office resources. His most recent compilation of the Lauds and Vespers books, which he worked on painstakingly, are nothing less than perfect—as in literally without error. I saw and held them with my own hands and was quite impressed by their flawless quality. An incredible asset to the community, Dom Myron tirelessly puts his heart and soul into enhancing the various aspects of the liturgy, which is such a high priority for the abbey.

✤ ✤ ✤

The afternoon weather has become somewhat predictable by now. By noontime, the rain started again, and through my office window I witnessed how the atmosphere transformed slowly into a gloomy scene.

While taking a couple of shots with my iPhone, as corny as it might sound, the classic Carpenters tune "Rainy Days and Mondays" kept ringing in my mind. I knew that if I had continued dwelling on it, it might have really gotten me down, as the song proclaims ("Rainy days and Mondays always get me down").

"Rainy Days and Mondays"

✣ ✣ ✣

To my puzzlement, I got an email from Philippine Airlines informing me that my rebooked flight for May 19 was changed to May 20—no further explanation. My only consolation was that it looked like my flight was at least still on, so I didn't bother to think much of it afterward.

✢ ✢ ✢

Before Vespers began, I watched with mild amusement from inside the chapel at Dom Arcadius and Dom John Paul sharing a medium-sized umbrella while ringing the bells in the rain. I couldn't resist taking a quick shot of them, which I then posted on Facebook with a caption that I composed to rhyme: "Rain or shine, the bells continue to ring, to get us ready for Vespers to sing!"

I think that not even a severe typhoon would deter the monks from proceeding with their liturgy. Of course, the rain only intensified the humidity inside the chapel, but with my vertigo spells now gone, it was more bearable.

✢ ✢ ✢

It's been another one of those warm nights. As I made my way back to my room after Compline, I passed through the now-familiar corridors, which I knew I'd miss, even as I counted my remaining days. And as if I hadn't taken enough photos of these hallways already, I took a few more. To me, their transcendent quietness struck me as pregnant with sacred meaning and stories. Staring at each of the corridors, I was consciously aware I was having my sentimental moment—what Pinoys term in the vernacular *sentimiento de bobo.*

 Their transcendent quietness struck me as pregnant with sacred meaning and stories.

12 MAY
tuesday

Monks' Blend Origin

Dom Jared and I arranged for another walk this morning after breakfast, but this time he asked Mark to join us. A twenty-one-year-old man, Mark used to teach in one of the diocesan Catholic schools in nearby Valencia City. As a new monk aspirant, he has recently been staying in the abbey as an observer. Now there are two of us non-monks regularly joining the liturgy.

With his long pants and Sunday shoes, Mark didn't strike me as properly attired for brisk walking. Sure enough, he and Dom Jared couldn't keep up with my fast pace. Both were so relieved each time I paused briefly to take pictures along the way. (I found out that I had gained quite the reputation among the monks as very "uncontemplative" in the way I walked—always rushing.)

Just before reaching the end of the old monastery road opening up to the main highway, we stopped by the old barn, where Dom Jared showed me the vast coffee plantation that the original monks had started cultivating in the early 1980s. The original plantation had occupied a few hectares and expanded considerably over the years.

The first coffee plantation near the monastery

Bukidnon's high altitude, cool climate, and rich volcanic soil have proven to be an ideal setting for growing coffee. I was told that from the late '80s to early '90s, when coffee prices plunged to an all-time low, the monks cooked up the idea of processing the coffee themselves. Thus a factory was erected and began its operations in May 1991, under the initial guidance and supervision of a Belgian consultant named Emil Baeyens (whose wife is a Filipina medical doctor in Malaybalay). The factory's first coffee roaster came from him—and is still in use today—and he taught the monks the mechanics of coffee roasting.

After three months of training and observing the coffee-roasting operation, the monks officially took over the factory in August 1991. Dom Carlo, a licensed chemical engineer, was assigned to be in charge of the factory as production supervisor, with Dom Myron and Dom Joseph assisting. In 1996, the factory was blessed to acquire an even bigger roaster, which was donated by Abbot Fidelis Ruppert and his monks from the Münsterschwarzach Abbey in Germany.

To this day, Monks' Blend coffee production and sales provide the majority of income for the abbey, supporting its various ministries. At the same time, the plantation and the factory continue to provide work for the locals of Malaybalay, which is in itself a ministry.

✢ ✢ ✢

When I got back to the abbey by midmorning, Roan, the monastery barber, was there attending to the monks, so I waited my turn to have another haircut with him. Since my hair has grown fast, I specifically instructed him to cut it even shorter than before, hoping there won't be a third time! In the back of my mind I was thinking, "This had better be the last, as I have no more hair dye left—and I don't want to ask the abbot for more!"

13 MAY
wednesday

Nouwen Connection

I was off to a super-early start, waking at 2 A.M. to catch the 3 A.M. Zoom book launch of Gabrielle Earnshaw's new release, *Henri Nouwen and the Return of the Prodigal Son: The Making of a Spiritual Classic.* The book launch featured Gabrielle herself, as well as Karen Pascal, the current executive director of the Henri Nouwen Society, and well-known author Fr. Ronald Rolheiser, also an avid Nouwen follower.

My very first introduction to Nouwen in 1993 was through his book *The Return of the Prodigal Son,* back when I was still a counseling student in the Philippines. Having been personally affected by Nouwen's spirituality and writing over the ensuing years, I've reckoned it part of my call to propagate his enduring spiritual legacy. Even CenterQuest carries the logo of Nouwen's favorite symbol of the wagon wheel with its emphasis on the hub, or the center. Having written four books on Nouwen between 2006 and 2015, and having conducted many retreats all over the United States and abroad focusing on his spirituality, I want to make sure I stay current on all things Nouwen. Never mind the time difference between Canada and the Philippines, I didn't want to miss this webinar. Despite the overly "contemplative" internet signal and poor connection in my room, the webinar was well worth waking up early for; the whole discussion validated my conviction that Nouwen's *Prodigal Son* book is indeed extraordinarily inspired, continuing to touch literally millions of people all over the world.

✦ ✦ ✦

At 7 A.M. I was all set to conduct our first Center-Quest School of Spiritual Direction Zoom applicant interview from the abbey since COVID-19 broke out. It was with an eighty-four-year-old woman from Ohio who is convinced that being a spiritual director is her ultimate calling for the remaining years of her life. After the lively interview the team unanimously discerned to accept this incredibly gifted and zealous woman into our upcoming cohort 5 cycle slated to begin in January 2021.

Soul companioning remains the most life-giving ministry I undertake. 🙶

By around 10 A.M., I was preparing for yet another Zoom call, this time with a spiritual directee from Los Angeles. No matter how busy I get, companioning people on their journey always takes priority in my schedule. There's nothing more fulfilling for me than to be with people, listen to their sacred stories, and accompany them on the path God establishes for them. More than teaching and leading retreats, both of which I immensely enjoy, soul companioning remains the most life-giving ministry I undertake.

✦ ✦ ✦

It had been a very long and exhausting day that began at 2 A.M., so as soon as Compline was over, I didn't think twice about going straight to my room without my usual stop at the Refectory for my hot tea. As I passed through the door of the monastery enclosure from the chapel, something that was hanging on the left wall just before the sacristy caught my eye, as if for the very first time. Emblazoned on a wooden panel was a familiar verse from Isaiah 30:15 that reads, "In quietness and trust is your strength." As I rested for the night, I claimed it as God's word for me.

 In quietness and trust is your strength.

The real Abbey Road

14 MAY
thursday

A Matter of Perspective

For the longest while I've been planning to capture a good picture of the main road fronting the Abbey Church, leading to the Abbey Gift Shop, before it turns left around the bend. I've imagined many times how I would compose the perfect shot in a way that would capture the road's mystique. But alas, each time I attempted it, there were vehicles parked near the guardhouse, or people hanging out there, or the weather was uncooperative—either the sun was glaring or the sky was too gloomy.

When I went outside to the road after morning Mass, I knew immediately the ideal time had finally come; the guardhouse was empty and the sky was bright and blue. Positioning myself right in the middle of the road, I aimed my iPhone to catch the road from the perfect perspective. I was proud of the result and captioned my Facebook post "The Real Abbey Road" (no apologies to the Beatles).

✦ ✦ ✦

My sunny disposition from this morning turned gloomy in an instant when I received two flight cancellation advisories, first from Philippine Airlines (PAL), then from Cebu Pacific Air, meaning my return trip is totally out of the picture. At lunch, the abbot first tried to console me and give me hope by suggesting that the abbey office could help me book an entirely new flight from Cagayan to Cebu, and Cebu to Los Angeles, without passing through Manila. For a while I harbored this possibility until it was confirmed that even Cebu was on strict lockdown, so there really was no way out for me.

Once more, some friends broached the idea of exploring the next available sweeper flight—which I previously brushed aside because of cost and timing, but mostly because of its overall uncertainty. Now, with my options running out, I had no choice but to reconsider the idea, especially after my friend Reyn, who is part of the Companions of the Redeemer and who works as a senior security investigator for the US Embassy in Manila, tipped me in advance about a sweeper flight projected to depart from Manila to Los Angeles on May 21. The only hitch was there was no domestic sweeper flight scheduled from Cagayan to Manila. Through his several connections, Reyn immediately put me in touch with the Department of Tourism (DOT) in Cagayan so I could further explore other options available for me.

In the next hour, I was on the phone with Blanche, a DOT representative who was able to get through to me via Viber on my US iPhone. (I didn't have a functioning local mobile phone with me, which added to my mounting distress.) She helpfully explained certain alternatives for both domestic and international flights, and called my attention to all the important travel requirements—including the mandatory health certificate from our local health center/city hall in Malaybalay—all of which struck me as complicated and time-consuming.

Meanwhile, Sr. M, through her sister Vem, connected me with a local PAL manager who could potentially help me with my tickets. I had to search for the PAL manager on Facebook and "friend" her so we could communicate via Facebook Messenger. Again I realized how critical it was to have a local mobile phone. I couldn't rely on any of the monks' phones for emergency use, since they are supposed to be turned off much of the time, especially when they are in prayer. I felt helpless, and I must confess, I considered borrowing any phone, even the abbot's, out of sheer desperation.

For the rest of the afternoon I was heavily preoccupied, trying to connect with people in the know—texting via Viber, Facebook Messenger, and WhatsApp in a frantic attempt to sort out my options, within the limited time frame. When I finally connected with Editha of PAL via Facebook Messenger, I thoughtlessly unloaded my frustrations on her and even implied that PAL was inflating ticket prices to take advantage of stranded folks like me. I only stopped my litany of grievances when I was confronted by a long pause on the other end of the line. That's when I detected Editha sobbing quietly.

Guilt-stricken, I immediately apologized for everything I had insensitively spilled out to her, especially after she disclosed to me that she had been working overtime as a manager, even without pay, trying to respond to all kinds of urgent travel needs, yet she felt very limited in what she could do. I had been so self-absorbed with my own pressing issues that I had failed to take into account that everybody was feeling the repercussions of the pandemic, one way or another, including PAL employees. In my heart, I felt very convicted for my inconsiderate attitude.

God knows how much I tried to squeeze whatever ounce of compassion and understanding I had left inside of me, but I was also on the verge of being disoriented on all fronts. The more I spoke to different people from different sectors, the more my confusion multiplied because of the tentative and sometimes even contradictory information I was collecting from them. I was close to throwing in the towel when the bell rang for Vespers.

✣ ✣ ✣

In anticipation of the Feast of St. Isidore (San Isidro), we had Vigils following Vespers. Toward the end of the service, I was taken by the unusually bright-colored sky outside as the evening was starting to fall. I had a visceral sense of foreboding in reaction to the splashes of red-orange, pink, and yellow hues; it looked to me like the sky was bleeding red, and I wasn't sure what to make of it. As usual, I made sure I documented the rare display with a couple of shots, and I posted them on Facebook. When the abbot commented afterward about my posts, it became clear to me that we were each viewing the same thing from an entirely different perspective. Ever the optimist, Abbot Ed expressed his reaction to the scene this way: "The red sky is very unusual. It also caught my attention. As if the sky is burning with the fire of the Spirit!" Amazing how the most dominant experience of your day can color your perception of reality!

15 MAY
friday

Positive Amid the Negative

Our morning at the abbey began with heavy fog on this feast day of San Isidro, the patron saint of Malaybalay. The whole area surrounding the church was thickly covered in misty white clouds. As expected, there wasn't the typical feasting, because of the pandemic. Without the usual local celebrations, the day just went by quietly, much like any other.

For me, life has to go on regardless of how despondent I am feeling inside. I admit, I even felt pressure to wear a happy face during the early morning School of Spiritual Direction interview we conducted with another applicant, who is based in South Korea. It was tough to balance being both authentic and self-controlled, but by the grace of God, I managed to give the interview the focus it deserved.

While the interview went fairly well, I could sense there was more going on than met the eye. When I reconnected with our interviewee later, I found out more about her qualms. I offered her ample space to further discern her own leaning and basically left the final decision up to her. This conversation confronted me once again with the striking reality that we are

211

indeed in the midst of tough times, when everybody seems to be in survival mode. On occasions like this, when I feel quite helpless, and when even my best efforts don't amount to much, I simply have to let go and choose to be OK with the situation as it is. Every act of releasing, I have to remind myself, is ultimately an act of trusting in a God who always knows better.

Every act of releasing ... is ultimately an act of trusting ...

✦ ✦ ✦

As I have been thinking about my complicated flight situation throughout the day, I've had this deep assurance that so many folks all over the world are covering me with their prayers. I just have to keep making the choice to keep my head above water, trusting that some viable solution will appear on the horizon at just the right time.

Meanwhile, even the Christian artist Amy Grant is calling my attention back to a much-needed state of groundedness. I stumbled upon her video on Facebook, in which she shared her way of grounding herself in God through a stillness practice that has proven helpful to her. Having been a fan of Amy's in my twenties (I still love her songs), I knew even back then that she had a contemplative side to her. Capping her meditation video with the phrase "We are loved!" I could only imagine Henri Nouwen applauding with grand approval. Way to go, Amy!

✦ ✦ ✦

It turned out I wasn't the only one nursing a heavy heart. Just a little over a week after losing a bonsai plant, another one disappeared at dawn this morning from the same location in the courtyard, according to

Fr. Elias, who was visibly upset and saddened when I spoke to him. Later, when I pressed him to share what he felt upon discovering this second loss, he texted me these words of quiet resignation:

> Feeling from the gut? Well, was wondering as 'twas unexpected ... but learned to let go of them after a while; things of this world are meant to be lost, so one need not cling to them but be detached. Of course, some things, even persons, have become part of you that sometimes it isn't easy to let go, but you just have to, in the process ... and be at peace!

I was not surprised to hear this from Fr. Elias, who always exudes an air of positivity—a powerful example for me.

✢ ✢ ✢

Speaking of something positive, amid all the other negative vibes I've been feeling lately, I received a piece of exciting news about my upcoming online course on Nouwen this July for Vancouver School of Theology:

> As of this morning's tally of Summer School registrations, your course is now a definite "go"—I will follow up in coming days about more details, but for now you have this good news. Your course, you may be happy to know, is drawing the largest numbers of registrations. I think Henri Nouwen's legacy is speaking particularly well to these unusual times.

My patron saint, Henri Nouwen, must be proud of me for perpetuating his spiritual legacy in the academy (my apologies for feeling self-congratulatory). I am just thrilled!

16 MAY

saturday

Thanks to God Indeed!

This Saturday was one of those days declared by the abbot as *Deo gratias* (literally, "thanks to God")—a day devoted to community or individual recreation where the monks engage in "talking meals" without the appointed readings and are free to attend to matters that need their attention. I've designated my whole day to firming up my plans to depart for the US by May 21. I've deliberately set my sights on ironing out all the kinks to ensure that my prospective trip will materialize.

First, I decided to take the chance and register for the sweeper flight with the US Embassy, to formalize my intent to depart on May 21 along with the other stranded US citizens and permanent residents. All I needed was PAL's approval and for them to contact me about ticketing procedures. Assuming I got the go-ahead, one problem remained: I had to get to Manila before the May 21 flight to Los Angeles, to pack up the belongings I left behind at the Companions of the Redeemer residence in Parañaque. Ideally that would mean reaching Manila at least a day before—or worst-case scenario, arriving the morning of May 21 and being ready to leave that same evening via the sweeper flight.

My only option—in the absence of a domestic sweeper flight—was to consider taking a military plane to Manila. Early on, my good friend Tom, a resident of Manila, volunteered to connect me with some of his military contacts, who might be able to help. Today I was directed by his contacts to seek clearance and representation from the Office of Civil Defense (OCD) so I could take the next scheduled military flight from Cagayan. Again, through the extra assistance of Reyn, I was able to email both the OCD main office in Manila and the regional one in Cagayan de Oro to request an official endorsement from them.

To my surprise, I received a series of email replies after a half hour: first, a standard response from the American Citizen Services (ACS) unit of the US Embassy; second, a simple acknowledgment email from the DOT Cagayan; third, a follow-up email from ACS InfoManila informing me that they were not in a position to help arrange for military flights, later confirmed by an Embassy officer; fourth, an email from OCD Manila detailing the requirements before facilitating anything through their OCD region in Cagayan; and finally, from OCD Cagayan acknowledging my request. Even with all these responses combined, I still didn't know quite how to proceed; I felt I wasn't really getting anywhere.

The only immediate thing I could work on was to secure a health clearance from the health center and city hall. Thank God for Dom Diego, who did all that on my behalf today. Because Malaybalay has no COVID-19 cases and Dom Diego knows all the right people there, the certificate was issued right away on the strength of his word, vouching that I've been inside the abbey the whole time, except for one short trip I made to Gaisano Mall, where I carried a Barangay clearance with me.

Throughout the day I was buried so deep in the task at hand that I hardly got up from my seat. Because of this I ended up missing most of the day's liturgy: midday prayer, Vespers, and Compline.

In the middle of all that, I got a call from a monk at the Manila Abbey early in the evening, expressing his concern for my situation. I had texted him, alerting him of my planned trip to Manila and exploring the possibility of me staying at the abbey there, which I thought would be safer than Parañaque, while waiting for my other flight to the US. I figured maybe I could request the Companions of the Redeemer guys to just pack up my belongings and bring them to the airport. In an apologetic but firm tone, the said monk enumerated his misgivings about my idea.

I needed no further convincing. I realized that this person was merely taking precautions for the sake of everyone in his abbey. I sincerely thanked him for his response, including our conversation in general, which touched on other areas I had not given serious thought. For instance, in taking a military flight, I hadn't even considered the kind of unregulated human contact I'd have with other passengers.

In hindsight, I appreciated the timely call as a definite godsend, for it put things in larger perspective for me. I'd been so driven to pursue whatever it took for me to get home to the States that I'd failed to calculate the risks involved in the process. The particular monk I spoke to did knock some sense into me through our divinely appointed conversation. I was forced to rethink my entire strategy. At the same time, I felt like I'd hit a wall, with no way out in sight.

There and then I rose from my chair and glanced at my watch to see if I could still catch the abbot after

Compline to seek his advice. When I reached his room, he had just gotten there. Seeing how flustered I appeared, he graciously let me in, and I wasted no time in telling him all that had transpired today. When I explained my current dilemma, he perfectly understood my position and affirmed everything the monk from Manila had said to me. In not so many words, he advised me to drop the military plane idea and wait for more viable options to open up in due time. He jokingly remarked that he'd rather see me stuck here in the abbey alive than for me to plunge into the unknown and end up dead.

Here in the abbey, the welcome would never end.

Hearing those sensible words from the abbot was a huge confirmation to me that the route I'd been pursuing might not be worth it after all. Still it meant more waiting for me—and who knew for how much longer. As if reading my worried mind, Abbot Ed assured me that here in the abbey, the welcome would never end. When I insisted that I'd already overstayed, he mildly rebuked me for being so Westernized in my thinking, reminding me that for Filipinos there is no such thing as overstaying. Even though I somehow knew that, I still needed to hear such reassurances that my stay would not inconvenience the abbey in any way. His last words before we said goodnight were music to my ears: "Wil, you blessed us, too, even as we blessed you." That was enough to usher me into a peaceful sleep.

Deo gratias, indeed!

17 MAY
sunday

More Than Words Can Say

It's a beautiful Sunday and I woke up clearheaded—like a load had been lifted from me. Here is God's incredibly timed message of assurance for me today from *TobyMac* via his Facebook blog:

> *If a door closes, quit banging on it.*
> *Perhaps it closed because*
> *you are worth so much more than*
> *what is on the other side.*

This reminds me of what Abbot Ed said to me last night—that he'd rather see me alive than dead.

Aside from the abbot and the monk in Manila I'd already spoke to, I consulted with three other friends about my case: Tom, Reyn, and Vic (one of the Manila oblates who was also trying his best to help me through his contacts with the Air Force). All of them validated the direction in which I was leaning, so I made my final decision to wait.

Aware that friends all over the world were tracking my situation and fervently praying for me, I issued this update on Facebook:

Dear Facebook Praying Friends:

I am deeply touched by the outpouring of prayer support you have extended to me. Yesterday was an agonizingly stressful day, to say the least. After hearing from the Embassy and the OCD and after serious consultation with five trusted friends whose opinions I greatly respect, including those going out of their way to help facilitate my departure, I have discerned with much peace that it's best for me to wait and not rush into trying to beat the May 21 sweeper flight.

In my eagerness to go home and grab the first open opportunity, I did put undue pressure on myself to make it happen, and it became clear to me last night that this may not be the best way to proceed. The risks involved far outweigh my perceived benefits and it may not be well worth it all. Anyhow, I wish I knew exactly what to do next except to say that I'll take things a step at a time with the light given me each day. I won't lie; this is tough for me, but I am choosing to wait—whatever, however, and wherever such waiting will take me! I don't know, but God does, and that is enough for me to keep trusting no matter what!

All in God's timing and perfect will (not Wil)!

Now that the issue is finally resolved, I am determined to chill out a bit after yesterday's chaotic episode. When Dom Carlo stopped by to deliver the ironed polo shirts to my room, I asked if he could show me around the backside of the monastery (to make sure I had company in the event that a cobra snake suddenly decided to make an appearance). Just when I thought I'd seen it all, there was one more corner left for me to discover on the vast monastery grounds. Thus I continued my never-ending explorations (and of course, picture taking) to document everything.

Close to the very edge of the monastery boundary where Dom Carlo showed me from a distance where the river flowed and the waterfalls were, I saw Dom Symeon and Pablita busily doing their yardwork at the back of the Oratory. What was once a densely weeded path filled with tall grasses growing in all sorts of unruly directions and dead branches scattered all over the area, has now been completely cleared. (I had proof of the transformation in the form of a "before" picture on my iPhone.)

Dom Symeon, dressed for some serious yard work, with his native hat on, looked like he was really in his element. I often witnessed him either raking the dried leaves or watering the plants. Once I checked out the monks' library in the basement of the Oratory, and I opened the sliding door leading to the backyard. There was Dom Symeon quietly tending to the plants and hosing them down in the scorching heat of the early afternoon sun.

Another time, walking through the hallway back to my room, I saw Dom Symeon doing what looked to me like a major cleaning job of the monks' common bathroom. Since it was during lockdown and the monastery workers had to work in shifts, he said it gave him a chance to help with cleaning chores in the abbey, which he considered a great stress reliever. (I wondered what might be stressing him out!)

Dom Symeon said in jest that he's decided to make a career out of his chosen *labora*—housekeeping and gardening. Well, as far as I can tell, he's doing a superb job! Maybe his love, especially of the outdoors and nature, is part of the Franciscan blood still flowing through his veins.

Dom Symeon, I learned, almost became part of the Order of Friar Minor, or OFM, a Franciscan order. Instead, as destiny would have it, he left OFM and entered the Benedictine abbey in Manila as a postulant in 1982. Eventually he joined the monks in Malaybalay as a novice in 1984, finally making his profession as a monk a year later. He was appointed as the prior of this same abbey in 2017.

Incidentally, I've often caught Dom Symeon eating boiled camote for breakfast. He developed this habit due to the influence of Fr. Col, who faithfully relied on the health benefits of camote, which can lower one's LDL ("bad" cholesterol), thus also diminishing the odds of potential heart issues, not to mention also lowering one's blood sugar, since boiled camote is low on the glycemic index. I must say, I never knew all those benefits, but nevertheless I personally never relished the idea of consuming boiled camote for early morning breakfast.

The other monk who gives me the impression of being health conscious is Fr. Elias. Once, he showed me his drink concoction—a mug full of soaked bright-blue flowers from the butterfly vine growing behind the cloister. Used medicinally for its anti-cancer properties primarily in Asia and Middle Eastern countries, this edible flower—known as *Clitoria ternatea*, or blue ternate—is said to be loaded with antioxidants and aids in collagen production (which prevents premature aging). Regular intake of this drink with a flower petal taste, it is claimed, helps improve one's eyesight, prevents hair loss, enhances memory, and boosts brain functioning, among other so-called benefits.

The ironic thing is, Fr. Elias, for all his devotion to this health drink, also loves drinking Coke, the benefits of which I'd be quick to question. I've gotten a kick out of teasing him about it (not to mention his preferences for certain not-so-healthy foods, which I've caught him gorging on). I guess all of us have our own proclivities!

✦ ✦ ✦

Before the close of this particular Sunday, I was
resting in my room waiting for the bell to ring for
Vespers when I thought of opening the sliding door
to my terrace for the very first time. Right outside
my room is a refreshing view of the grassy field with
towering trees lined up majestically against the
wide-open sky. I didn't even need to step outside to
enjoy the sight of the lush green trees and appreciate
the natural beauty surrounding me. I must already
be so habituated to my environment that I tend to
take little blessings such as this for granted.

| View of towering trees in luscious green

A line from "The Measure of the Fullness," a song
composed by Mark Beazley, a former student of mine
and upcoming participant in our School of Spiritual
Direction cohort 5, kept ringing in my ears:

*"As the evening falls,
we recount your goodness!"*

I felt immensely favored—and, as the title of Mark's album puts it, "more than my words can say!"

18 MAY
monday

Monday Morning Stroll

Today is my wife Juliet's sixty-first birthday—the third occasion for which I've been absent from home. I've come to fully accept that I might not be home for another month or so, depending on what opens up for me, which I've decided is no longer worth worrying about.

To take my mind off any more thoughts of home, I decided to take a walk. It wasn't all that hard to entice Dom Jared and Mark to accompany me in exploring the other side of the monastery—the opposite direction from the rice fields (around Villa Arcadio, as the area was called)—with unpaved dirt roads that are slightly muddy from the rains that have visited us fairly regularly.

Together, the three of us embarked on our morning walk. It was more of a leisurely walk this time, which my two companions likely much preferred. At one point on our walk, from a spot overlooking the nearby highway, Dom Jared called our attention to a Jollibee restaurant (the McDonald's of the Philippines, only better, in my not-so-humble opinion). If only I had my wallet with me, I wouldn't have thought twice about heading there and treating Dom Jared and

Mark to yet another Pinoy breakfast. I missed eating at Jollibee (the real Pinoy one, not the stateside one).

Feeling deprived of the Jollibee prospect, we settled on an alternative route and proceeded to explore the various wooded interior roads and bamboo-strewn pathways, while I captured with my iPhone the panoramic views of the mountain and the sky, savoring every imaginable angle. I even made sure to pose for a quick photo by the window of an old abandoned hut, which almost collapsed the moment I stepped inside. After about an hour and a half we took a shortcut back to the abbey, which was just as scenic. What an energizing morning well spent! Going straight to the Refectory, I was eager to check what our midmorning snack might be.

Sacred grounds around the abbey

✢ ✢ ✢

I **found out** that Dom Diego went to town to update our certificates of clearance for extended coverage dates, including Loury's and Dom Carlo's (who had volunteered in advance to accompany me in case we had to leave for the airport in Cagayan at any time). This he did on his own initiative, which I so appreciated, in light of his many other demanding responsibilities in the abbey.

Dom Diego, a native of Cebu, acts as the farm manager in charge of overseeing the workforce for the coffee, cacao plantations, and rice fields, including managing the cattle owned by the abbey—a very big job, I could only imagine. On top of all that, he does the food and grocery shopping every Saturday, and serves every night as the designated cantor for Compline. Dom Diego actually possesses a good singing voice. When I complimented him for it, he self-effacingly downplayed it.

I'd met Dom Diego a few years ago, before my first visit to the abbey, when he attended one of my weekend Nouwen retreats at Our Lady's Hill Spirituality Center in Negros Occidental. It's only now that I've come to know him, in the context of his responsibilities at the Refectory, as a person who is quite pleasant in a quiet sort of way.

One time I caught Dom Diego preparing a Jell-O dessert in the kitchen, which I happened to like. (I have a nose for anything sweet!) Again, when I complimented him about it, he explained, in an almost apologetic tone, that he was simply trying to concoct something out of whatever ingredients were left in the pantry. Well, it must've turned out well because that night, when the milky Jell-O was served after dinner to the monks, it was gone just like that. (I regretted only tasting a bit of it.)

Another time I saw Dom Diego at the Refectory in a peculiarly quiet mood, looking a bit pale and somewhat downcast. When I asked if something was the matter, he complained about feeling bloated and experiencing stomach cramps. His face lit up when I offered him what was left from my GutConnect 365 dietary supplement, which I brought with me from the States. Whether or not that helped ease his discomfort that day, I never found out. I could only hope it did.

19 MAY
tuesday

Open Door

This morning I received a text from Dinah, a friend from Davao City who now lives with her family in Bakersfield, California. Unbeknownst to me, she has also been stranded while vacationing in Davao. Dinah informed me that there was a sweeper flight to Los Angeles scheduled for May 26. I was quick to correct her by insisting that the May 26 flight was headed to San Francisco, which was why I ignored it the first time I heard about it. (Who wanted to fly to San Francisco and then take another flight to Los Angeles?) She swore that she'd just gotten an email earlier that morning confirming that the flight was to LA. Sensing that I was incredulous, she forwarded the actual advisory from the US Embassy. I couldn't believe my eyes when I saw that she was absolutely correct. What's more, the advisory stated that there also was a domestic sweeper flight leaving from Cagayan to Manila on the same day.

My heart skipped a beat. I took the chance and registered online with the Embassy for both domestic and international flights. Dinah and I covenanted to pray for each other that Philippine Airlines would contact us right away, although I still had my doubts based on my last experience with the airline.

Slightly apprehensive yet excited at the same time, I posted an update on Facebook, in an effort to mobilize as many prayer warriors as I could to intercede on my behalf. (Yes, I knew I could count on a number of my Facebook friends to pray for me.) When I finally surrendered everything to God, what I thought was already a closed door suddenly swung wide open, and I chose to believe that this must be a God thing.

> *What I thought was already a closed door suddenly swung wide open ...* "

Important Update and Prayer Request

A sweeper flight opened up for May 26 from CDO to MLA and leaving on the same day from MLA to LA. I just registered through the Embassy/PAL partnership this morning. Pray that PAL approves it and contacts me right away to confirm. Pray too that I'd have a little window in between arrival to and departure from MLA to unpack/repack in Parañaque (more than half my stuff is there to be sorted out). Regardless, if this is an open door, things will really fall into place! Many thanks in advance!

"Lord, pave the way if this is in line with Your timing and will!"

20 MAY
wednesday

"O God, Come to My Aid"

I waited the entire morning for a call from PAL but nothing came. Wary that I might miss this new opportunity, I consulted Blanche from the DOT about how to ensure that I got counted in for the two sweeper flights on May 26. Her response was swift and definitive: I should go personally to Cagayan to purchase my tickets at the local PAL office so my fate could be sealed once and for all. I trusted Blanche, so I was more than willing to take such a risk.

When my original flight was first cancelled, I had to purchase a new ticket to rebook, which was more than double the amount of my one-way return ticket. This time I was hoping that PAL would honor my already-paid ticket and just add my new domestic reservation and make up whatever difference there might be with the new price. Since I've been away for nearly four months now, my finances were not in good shape, so I had to request my sons to fund my checking account in the event I got charged for a brand-new ticket.

Thank God our clearance documents were ready; bless Dom Diego for speedily working on them last

Monday! I made immediate arrangements with Dom Carlo to accompany me to Cagayan early tomorrow. Loury would be our driver. Despite all the advanced preparations I've made, I didn't want to leave any stone unturned, so I still planned on contacting the PAL hotline before the day was over, upon the advice of Blanche. Knowing how phone hotlines work (or don't work), I borrowed Dom Carlo's mobile phone, loaded it with enough prepaid minutes, and scheduled my call right after Compline.

I prepared myself for a long, extended call with PAL, and after being passed on from one customer representative to another, I finally landed with a so-called PAL specialist whose well-rehearsed line each time he returned after putting me on hold went like this: "Thanks for your patience; I apologize for the delay." The last wait lasted for almost forty-five minutes, only for the specialist to inform me that I wasn't on the list of PAL-approved passengers for the domestic and international flights leaving on May 26. To which I responded—without any hint of panic on my part—that a DOT representative assured me that I could simply proceed to our local ticketing office (Cagayan) the next day so I could be added to the list. His reply pushed my panic button a bit. The specialist couldn't assure me that the local office in Cagayan would even be open to the public. I refused to engage him any further and just thanked him and hung up.

Instead, I decided to believe Blanche from the DOT, whom I recalled telling me that she would be in the PAL office the following day. I knew it could be a risk to drag Dom Carlo and Loury all the way to Cagayan only discover that the PAL office was closed, but there was no turning back now (it was late in the evening and there was no way we could find out for sure, and we were already set to leave after the morning Mass the next day).

Before finally calling it a night, I could only echo the Psalmist's prayer that we always recite during Lauds:

"O God, come to my aid;
O Lord make haste
to help me!"

This is such an overly familiar prayer whose urgent tone has taken on a new meaning for me in light of my time-sensitive situation.

21 MAY
thursday

Curtailed Joy

After grabbing a quick breakfast as soon as the morning Mass was over at 6 A.M., I took off on the two-and-a-half-hour drive to Cagayan de Oro City with Dom Carlo and Loury, passing through certain checkpoints without any problem. To my great relief, as we arrived at the PAL office, we saw the office was indeed opening at 8:30 A.M. I was in fact the very first in line when the door finally opened, and the whole ticketing process went smoothly—without me having to shell out money for an entirely new ticket but just adding a few hundred dollars more to cover the difference between my cancelled ticket and my new domestic ticket.

In less than an hour with the PAL agent, we were out of the office with my domestic and international tickets in hand, along with the assurance that my name had been officially added to the list of sweeper-flight passengers departing Cagayan for Manila and Manila for Los Angeles on May 26. On our way out, Blanche approached me and introduced herself. Finally I got to meet her face to face after our many conversations over Viber for the past several days. I was, of course, extremely thankful to her for facilitating everything for me. Thank God I'd heeded her advice; otherwise I would probably still be waiting for PAL to contact me.

All Dom Carlo, Loury, and I could think of next was where we could have lunch before heading back to the abbey. Volunteering to treat both of them, I asked what their preference was. Loury suggested a place called "Pinutos sa Canto" (Wrap Around the Corner), a favorite stop for the monks when picking up people at Laguindingan International Airport, near Cagayan, to go to the abbey. I first sampled their menu back in 2017, when Fr. Col brought us there late at night, coming from the airport with my friends from Chicago, Jim and Jerry Lee. (Jerry is a graduate of our CenterQuest School of Spiritual Direction inaugural cohort.) I was there again the following year and I'd had some bad stomach problems afterward.

So when Loury brought up the idea of going to Pinutos, I wasn't sure how to respond because the mere mention of it made me quickly lose my appetite. I kept quiet for a while, waiting for the right moment to suggest an alternative. Then I remembered our aborted Jollibee outing from last week. At the risk of sounding selfish, I raised the Jollibee option, which both of them agreed to without apparent misgivings. (I later found out that Loury was allergic to chicken, so he was very limited in his menu options.)

As soon as we located a Jollibee branch near the highway, we ordered at the drive-through and then searched for a convenient spot on the safe side of the main road to park our van and enjoy our food unhurriedly. Here I was, wanting to give Dom Carlo and Loury a little treat for something they liked, but instead we ended up settling for what I preferred. I felt bad for Loury, especially because, if I remembered correctly, he didn't even like spaghetti, so there wasn't much choice for him but to order a burger. Dom Carlo seemed content with his order, as I was. We capped off our meals with the famous Jollibee peach mango pie for dessert.

I must've dozed off a few times on the long drive back to the abbey. At one point I overheard Loury talking on his cell phone with somebody from the abbey, but I didn't know who it was or what it was about until we received an unexpected "advisory" from Dom John Paul (the abbey nurse), who was waiting for us at the administration building when we arrived. As soon as we alighted from the van, he told us that we needed to quarantine, since we had gone to Cagayan, which was a COVID-19-infected city.

At first I thought Dom John Paul was pulling my leg; he'd been aware of this trip beforehand. But it didn't take me long to figure out that he was actually serious in wanting to quarantine Dom Carlo and me. In fact, he proceeded to suggest that I transfer from the cloister to one of the rooms in the guest house, where Dom Carlo was presently staying.

Dom Carlo didn't say much, but I could tell he didn't appreciate this surprise news either. However, while he was upset about it, at the same time he seemed only too willing to submit to the quarantine, for that meant an additional break from the abbey. (He had actually gone on a self-imposed quarantine for twelve days right after Easter Sunday because of his incessant coughing. He enjoyed the restful break from his abbey responsibilities, not just as a guest master but also as one of the cantors during the liturgy, not to mention serving as the personal secretary of the abbot.)

When it became evident to me that Dom John Paul was quite keen on imposing the quarantine, I bargained with him to at least allow me to stay where I was in the enclosure and not move to the guest house, since I only had five remaining days before I was to depart. On the strict condition that I wouldn't show up during liturgy and would endeavor to distance myself from any of the monks, Dom John Paul allowed me to settle back into my room in the cloister.

I think the full impact of this sudden development didn't really sink in for me until later. That evening, as I rested, one by one the implications of such an abrupt decision slowly hit me. First, I felt like I'd been doused with cold water after the triumph of securing my tickets back to the States, which I considered a major cause for celebration. Second, the very thought of being isolated from all the monks during the last five days of my stay saddened me terribly. Finally, this was not the kind of culminating episode I had envisioned before finally leaving the abbey; it felt like a cruel ending.

True, I was being emotional. Aware of the mix and range of my fluctuating feelings, I was careful not to allow their power to rule me. As a way of letting them go—or perhaps more truthfully, trying to muffle my frustration—I lay down in bed for a while to rest my weary body and my clouded mind, staring blankly on the ceiling until my eyes slowly closed on their own.

✦ ✦ ✦

As directed, I did not show up for Vespers and Compline that evening. Before going to bed, I texted Abbot Ed, partly to fill him in on what had transpired during our trip and partly to ask his permission to go to my office tomorrow to use the internet, away from where the monks usually were (my subtle way of hinting about our quarantine situation). His response took me by surprise. Without much elaboration, he alluded to his intent to modify the restrictions just handed down to us.

Next thing I knew, there was a text from Dom John Paul conveying the abbot's instructions to limit our quarantine to twenty-four hours and lifting all the other restrictions, provided I took a long bath and washed my used clothes thoroughly. Dom John Paul punctuated his text to me with a sincere apology, in case he had inadvertently caused me any discomfort—a humble move on his part that I greatly appreciated.

I responded as honestly as I could by admitting to him that I'd been taken aback and that I couldn't agree with the reasoning behind it. However, I assured him that I wasn't begrudging him for anything as I was convinced that he really meant well, even if his mandate struck me as over the top or overkill. Sure, I was upset by the situation, but truthfully I wasn't upset with Dom John Paul himself, who had gone out of his way to help me a few times—buying me medicines and other personal items.

Never once did I doubt the purity of Dom John Paul's intention, which I knew was meant for the highest good of everyone. My initial reactions were something I took ownership and responsibility for as they expressed more my own issues than his—reactions that really arose from my sentimental feelings of possibly leaving the abbey without having the opportunity to properly say goodbye to all the monks. While I ended my text to Dom John Paul truly appreciating his efforts, I did entertain some second thoughts about how he might have received the frank tone with which I relayed my sentiments. Time and again, I have to remind myself that my Americanized directness may not sit well with Pinoy sensitivities. And Dom John Paul struck me as one of those sensitive souls, so I felt a bit guilty afterward.

Dom Carlo's reaction to the relaxation of the quarantine was another story. He insisted on continuing his self-quarantine at the guest house, for reasons that made me smile with a bit of amusement. However, he assured me that he would accompany me to the airport on May 26, in case I ran into any emergency issues in connection with my departure.

Zoom Packing

This was the first post I made on Facebook this Friday morning; "God did come to my aid and the Lord did hasten to help me. Thanks be to God!" I confidently announced to the world, with my two flight tickets in hand, that I was finally going home on May 26—in exactly four days! As my final tribute to my extended time in the monastery, I also posted the latest slideshow video I made, entitled "Sacred Grounds," which is a collection of my best nature shots of the abbey's surroundings, taken mostly while walking with Dom Jared and Mark over the past month.

As I count my last remaining days at the abbey and savor my experience of the past two months before I return home to the US, I am all the more convinced that should God indeed favor us with the CenterQuest-Asia launch of our School of Spiritual Direction program sometime in the next two to three years, we would definitely aim to conduct our eight-day closing residency at the Abbey of the Transfiguration so that our inaugural cohort participants can be exposed to the monastic rhythm and the experience of Benedictine hospitality. Even now, I've started seriously praying for what I am envisioning for CQ-Asia to materialize, all in God's perfect time—with the abbey playing a major part in the residential component of our program.

✦ ✦ ✦

Because my domestic and international flights on May 26 are considered connecting flights, with a very short window in between, I am left without much option but to leave many of my belongings at the Companions of the Redeemer (COR) residence in Parañaque and take back with me to Los Angeles only what I absolutely need. Since I can't be sure whether I will be allowed to check additional luggage while passing through the Manila International Airport, I have to play it safe and settle for a small carry-on suitcase.

There I was at 10 A.M., all set to Zoom with Alfie and Dave, two of the COR guys who live at the house where I left behind three suitcases, a few boxes of assorted material, several pairs of shoes, some clothes, and some unsorted retreat paraphernalia. The guys had everything ready to be sorted in their living room, just waiting for my specific instructions. For the next hour, we went through every item from the suitcases and the boxes, and I made on-the-spot decisions which ones to repack and which to leave behind. Dave even used a scale to make sure we weren't going over the carry-on weight limit. I couldn't believe I was actually packing long distance via Zoom with other people doing it on my behalf. Yet Dave, Alfie, and I did it together successfully—and had fun!

All said and done, it wasn't that difficult for me to let go of various items, including clothes, shoes, personal effects, souvenir gifts, and so on. It was enough of a victory for me to finally be returning home. Somehow we just need to coordinate and time the hand-off perfectly at the Ninoy Aquino International Airport between my domestic arrival and my international departure on May 26.

The best part of it—and so impeccably timed—is that Reyn, one of the other COR guys, will also be at the airport in his capacity as diplomatic security for the US State Department, assigned to support the American foreign service officers who are providing US citizen services via the sweeper flights. All in all, I have confidence that everything is finally falling into place.

 It was enough of a victory for me to finally be returning home.

Showers of blessings |

23 MAY
saturday

Showers of Blessings

To echo the old popular tune by the legendary singer-songwriter John Denver, "All my bags are packed, I'm ready to go" ("Leaving on a Jet Plane"). I was so all set and raring to leave that I was literally counting not just the few days but the hours I've got left before my final departure. Unlike the song lyrics, I know when I'll be back again to the abbey—God willing, next year's Holy Week.

In fact, to lighten my luggage a bit (and allow room for a few more souvenir gifts for friends), I chose to leave some of my things (walking shoes and a few clothes) with Dom Carlo for next year's anticipated return.

Early in the afternoon, I was able to swing by the Abbey Gift Shop for my final chance to buy a few more things just before we experienced another heavy rain. Soon I found myself quietly watching the rain fall—which I welcomed as heavy showers of blessings.

Ascension Sunday Mass

24 MAY
sunday

CenterQuest Musings

Today was the Ascension Sunday in the abbey, even though the celebration of the Ascension of our Lord traditionally falls on a Thursday (forty days after Easter). In attendance on this special Sunday were both the Blue Sisters and Green Sisters, as well as some of the abbey regulars, whom I noticed were gradually increasing in numbers—and still practicing proper social distancing. Though still far from what it used to be, the Mass celebration is slowly starting to look and feel more normal again, just when I am about to leave the abbey.

Performing during the Mass was the Men's Choir—their first appearance since the lockdown restrictions in the abbey began. What a treat it was for me to hear them sing again on my last Sunday here! I'd almost forgotten what a huge difference a choir makes in enhancing people's worship experience.

The present Men's Choir emerged out of the original Boys' Choir formed in 1990 by Fr. Benildus Maramba, OSB, of the Manila Abbey, who took up residence at the Abbey of the Transfiguration for a year. He devoted his time to training the choir members, who eventually became well-known performers.

(They even did a series of concerts in California in 1995 and 1999, sponsored by the Sisters of Social Service.) From the pioneer group composed of twenty-four boys ages ten to twelve years old, a few continued on as part of the Men's Choir, which still sings regularly during the Monks' Conventual Mass thirty years later and is a regular feature in the abbey during Holy Week and other special occasions.

Right after morning Mass, I attended the final three Zoom meetings scheduled for each of the three small groups participating in our May Soul Companioning class with CenterQuest. I could not afford to miss any of them because, in my opinion, this May batch was the most diversified group of participants we've ever had in the thirty times we've run this four-week introductory course. Their high level of engagement was unsurpassed. It was also the largest class we've had since we launched the course back in 2014, which is why we appointed cofacilitators for each of the three groups for the first time.

All members of the three groups were very transparent and vulnerable in their sharing—even more remarkable within the context of a virtual community—and the bonding within each group was extraordinarily strong. Since day one, I'd somehow had a sense that this class could potentially yield the highest number of qualified applicants for the upcoming cohort 5 of our CenterQuest School of Spiritual Direction (CQ SSD), and I made sure that my three cofacilitators and I invested the focused time and energy that this group deserved.

✤ ✤ ✤

I finally finished videotaping myself for one last time from the abbey. In the video I issued a fresh invitation to our target group to take a serious step of faith toward applying for our January 2021 cohort 5—even in the face of the pandemic, economic challenges, and all the other unknowns before us—should any of them sense a strong calling from God to pursue this direction for their lives and ministry.

The video presentation was brief and to the point, but it felt good for me to be able to convey CQ's deep commitment to moving forward with our projections for cohort 5, despite all the present challenges. What initially prompted this video was the inactivity in our SSD application process over the past couple of months, since the pandemic has escalated. With the application deadline coming up soon, I felt a compelling urge to address the urgency of the matter head-on, so that CQ would have a better idea of where we stood and what we could realistically expect.

> *I wish to get across ... our ultimate decision to fully trust God ...*

From my perspective, posting this video is critical in terms of CQ's overall timetable. As the executive director, I am counting on this initial move to firmly seal the general direction we are taking by faith.

The chief message I wish to get across to our constituency is our ultimate decision to fully trust God with what might seem impossible from a strictly human standpoint, given the continuing uncertainties of the pandemic. I plan to post the video on my various social media platforms first thing tomorrow, which will be the day before my departure from the abbey.

Inside the Abbey Church

The monks during liturgy

Farewell, Dear Abbey

We celebrated this morning's Mass in honor of the venerable St. Bede, the patron saint of the San Beda schools run by the Benedictines of the Abbey of Our Lady of Montserrat in Manila—the same abbey where Abbot Ed first served as abbot for six years. The Manila abbey conducts their own celebration during every opening of a new school year—usually sometime in August or September—to acquaint all the incoming students of San Beda University and San Beda College with their patron saint.

St. Bede (San Beda in Spanish) was an English Benedictine monk whose most famous work, *Ecclesiastical History of the English People*, earned him the title "The Father of English History." Considered one of the greatest teachers and writers of the early Middle Ages, and regarded by many historians as the most important scholar of antiquity, St. Bede remains the only Englishman conferred the title Doctor of the Church, by Pope Leo XIII in 1899.

✧ ✧ ✧

As planned, I released my CenterQuest School of Spiritual Direction video today on all my different social media accounts, hoping that God will use this special medium of communication to directly speak to the people whose hearts God has already been preparing to come on board with us. Over time I've learned, again and again, that God handpicks folks who are perfectly compatible with what we have to offer at CQ, including those I might not have guessed would thrive richly in our CQ soil. Conversely, some that I would've predicted as a great fit for our program sometimes struggle heavily through the application process, whether it's because of issues with the interview, scheduling conflicts, funding, visa status, or any number of other reasons.

> *It is God who brings us the right people in God's own time.*

It's tough to let go when you're invested in certain individuals who are full of potential, in terms of your own desires for them, only to discover that their chances of succeeding on your envisioned path for them may turn out to be unlikely, for reasons that are difficult to fathom at times. One would think that after having been on this road several times before, I would've learned these lessons well—but I continue to relearn them, and I must keep reminding myself that ultimately it is God who brings us the right people in God's own time. And my precise prayer after sending and posting my recent video is one consciously aligned with this freshly anchored perspective—a surrender borne out of my focused time here at the abbey.

✣ ✣ ✣

To serve as my official abbey farewell announcement to everyone who has been following my monastery saga, I came up with an updated eight-minute slide-show video version of "Dear Abbey" and posted it on my own Facebook timeline and on our Benedictine Friends group page. In watching the video for the nth time, my heart couldn't contain my overflowing gratitude for the tremendous gift this abbey has been to me.

✧ ✧ ✧

Here I recount some of the more mundane impressions I've had during my stay in the abbey that might seem inconsequential for others but will surely remain with me whenever I look back on my experience with the community as an accidental monk:

• Watching Dom John Paul, Dom Arcadius, and Dom Jared pull the ropes of the bell tower effortlessly for ten minutes straight, rain or shine, before every Lauds and Vespers

• Hearing the loud—and regular—belching of Fr. Elias, as if he has a bean in his throat during liturgy

• Seeing Dom Pietro enjoy his favorite Nutella spread on his bread almost every breakfast (until the jar is empty)

• Noticing Dom Symeon's slightly (but perennially) late entrance by the left side of the church during most morning Masses (he surely must have good reasons that I just never found out)

• Witnessing Fr. Col position himself regularly on the edge of the corridor basking in the midday sunlight (for his much-needed vitamin D)

• Overtaking Fr. Elias consistently as I'd rush

toward the chapel to attend Lauds very early in the morning, while he slowly makes his way through the corridor, praying the Rosary

· Encountering Dom Myron quietly, our eyes not meeting, as he stops, without fail, by the Confession and Counseling Room's restroom just before Lauds

· Overhearing the sounds of laughter next door to my office in the Abbey Administration Building, with Dom Symeon often engaging in lively exchanges with the office women while enjoying snacks with them

· Witnessing the abbot next door to my office deep in contemplation—checking his Facebook

✦ ✦ ✦

Before and after Vespers I couldn't resist—one last time before taking off tomorrow morning—taking several photos of the magnificent view of the skies above the Abbey Church and the Refectory area. It was like an unbounded canvas laid out against the sky being painted dramatically in variegated style. Without a doubt, I would miss the wide-open skies of Bukidnon. There's nothing like it anywhere else I know—not as magically enchanting as here in Malaybalay, evoking in me a spontaneous note of praise to our God. In this particular moment, one of my favorite responsorial chants from the liturgy at Saint Andrew's Abbey came to mind: "The splendor of his name reaches far beyond heaven and earth" (cf. Ps

> *The splendor of his name reaches far beyond heaven and earth.* ""

148:13). I couldn't help but hum its melody quietly as I made my way inside the Refectory.

When the bell rang afterward, I joined the monks for my "last supper" with them. The abbot called on me when the farewell dinner was over to briefly address the community one last time. With mixed emotions, I once more expressed my heartfelt gratitude to each of the monks present for the unparalleled hospitality I have received from them throughout my extended stay.

I don't think it's strange to say that it was for me both a sad and joyful evening!

| The monastic community

26 MAY
tuesday

Home At Last

I had my last Lauds and Mass with the monks this morning, then said my final goodbyes, rolled my luggage out of my room, and loaded everything into the van parked outside the guest house, with Loury's help. Dom Carlo had Manman prepare a special breakfast for us, which even included my favorite garlic shrimp dish, to my surprise! At 8 A.M. I was already on the road with Dom Carlo and Loury, heading straight to Cagayan de Oro's Laguindingan International Airport, which we reached in a record time of less than three hours, passing through one checkpoint after another with no delays.

Dom Carlo and Loury decided to stand by in the parking lot while I was going through the preliminary clearance procedures with the local Department of Tourism—again, Blanche was present—and the Department of Health. As soon as I reached the ticket counter, I texted Dom Carlo thanking him and assuring him that all was clear and they could now leave.

I was surprised by the number of stranded passengers crowding the airport, apparently flying to destinations other than Los Angeles. With the added perk of being a senior citizen and enjoying my priority lane privileges, my airport routine proceeded with remarkable ease, except for a slight delay in our departure for Tagbilaran, Leyte in the Visayas, where we had to make a short stopover before continuing our flight to Manila.

By 2 P.M. I was starving, but unexpectedly, several PAL stewardesses showed up and began distributing complimentary snacks at the boarding area: a brownie bite the size of a peso, a very cute *mamon* (like a sponge cupcake), and a bottled water. Thank you, Philippine Airlines!

But with such tiny portions of snacks, I was still quite hungry, so I had no choice but to open a pack of the Monks' Roasted Peanuts, meant as part of my pasalubong for the COR guys who were planning to meet me at the Ninoy Aquino International Airport (NAIA) with the carry-on luggage they had packed for me. I jokingly texted to alert them to what I had just resorted to—complete with photographic evidence—knowing they'd understand.

Our sweeper plane finally landed at NAIA Terminal 2 at around 6:30 P.M., and after another round of luggage inspection we were shuttled to Terminal 1 where Alfie, Dave, and Reyn were patiently waiting for me with my luggage. After a couple of selfie souvenir shots together, Reyn, using all his embassy connections, escorted me directly to the PAL ticket counter (skipping the long queue of passengers), where I was able to check my carry-on bag.

Overflowing with gratitude for all that the COR gang had done to help with my departure at NAIA, Reyn and I parted ways before I entered the immigration area. Just twenty-five minutes before the gate closed, I reached the boarding area for my Los

Angeles flight. And when I got on the plane, who was sitting right next to me but my friend Dinah, whom God had used to prompt me to register for a spot for this sweeper flight! How each and every minute detail has fallen into perfect place can only be divine engineering. As I look back on everything, it's absolutely mind-boggling!

Normally I have trouble sleeping well during a long flight such as this one, but I must've been that fatigued, because for the most part, I managed to steal some good chunks of restful sleep throughout the fourteen-hour direct flight. To my shame, despite all the wide-open doors I've already smoothly passed through, I still caught myself entertaining the fear that I might be mandated to quarantine when I arrived at the Los Angeles airport, or even hit with some other unexpected roadblock. But all my fears turned out to be unfounded as I breezed through immigration and customs without any bother. With my luggage in hand, I came out of the Tom Bradley International arrival terminal just in time for my son Jonathan to pick me up.

> *I was … overcome with an ineffable sense of God's faithfulness and love …*

In that moment, as I stood outside at the passenger pick-up area waiting for my son to show up, I was all of a sudden overcome with an ineffable sense of God's faithfulness and love enveloping me ever so tightly through everything that I have experienced since I'd left Los Angeles almost four months ago. And now, after all that never-ending waiting, I was back home at last.

To God be the glory!

epilogue

I left Manila on the morning of Tuesday, May 26 (which was the afternoon of Monday, May 25, California time) and arrived in Los Angeles still on May 26, in the evening. Being so acclimated to traveling between the Philippines and the United States for many years, the day and night time differences had hardly been an issue for me. But because I'd been gone for four months, with more than two months of those confined to a singular location, I felt the effect intensely for the first time in a long while. It wasn't just the abrupt change in my body clock that had me reeling but also the rapid break from the monastic rhythm I'd been in, and I felt it for at least a week after I got back.

Oddly enough, but thankfully, I got over the hump of inertia and managed to bounce back relatively quickly, thanks in large part to the mounting demands of my work with CenterQuest and a ton of urgent domestic concerns. Soon I was back to the daily grind and my California routine as though I had never left America.

Once I made up my mind to commit to this diary project, I began reconstructing the contents and chronology of my abbey experience. Never before had I worked on a writing task this fast, and I couldn't hold back the burst of energy I was experiencing as I kept pushing myself, night and day, to attend to it, on top of all my other demanding responsibilities. By mid-July I was done with the first draft of two and a half months' worth of diary entries.

To attribute my high energy to mere inspiration would not be wholly accurate; I have genuinely felt a strong inner summons to chronicle my monastic experience, which is still so palpable to me. Never in any of my prior work have I expressed such a high degree of openness, transparency, and vulnerability. I became convinced that I do have a story to tell, and that I am willing to go on record and share it with the world. Yet it's not only my story but a shared story of my life intersecting with the life of a community that has profoundly readjusted and expanded my own views of spirituality, theology, ministry, and community life.

I trust you will catch a glimpse of these evolving views from my daily diary accounts, which include the various issues I wrestled with along the way, as I confronted them both directly and indirectly. Frankly, at this stage in my life, I no longer feel as threatened as I used to about espousing a more open view of the spiritual life. As a result of this openness, I can also sense a continual broadening of my spiritual convictions—as opposed to their confinement, which would only lead to my own stagnation. This radical stance has already proven to be a very freeing path for me to take.

As an oblate, the Benedictine environment is not at all alien to me. On my own I have even done some basic studies in monastic spirituality. But being thrust into monastic community life on a daily basis for a period of time was a different experiment altogether. In a relatively brief span of time I learned, through firsthand experience, what books and my intermittent brushes with monasticism could not possibly teach me. I have been so lucky for the privilege to experience this monastic community in its natural setting, which has radically altered the romanticized version that I had subconsciously held before.

I came to this community with the purpose of teaching Benedictine spirituality during Holy Week, and instead ending up being taught by the monks, through their living example, the Benedictine virtues of stability, obedience, and conversion. As I have surveyed my time at the abbey, I have come to deepen my resolve to convey to a wider audience, through this diary, what it's like to embrace an everyday spirituality, based on what I have gleaned from this community and what I have learned from my own personal struggles of living out its reality.

My aim in publishing this diary is not merely to provide you with an inside look at monastic life—as fascinating as that may be for many—or at my ongoing wrestling to live out my own spiritual life within such setting during my period of strandedness. Yes, I have written about all that, but I also wish to go beyond. The series of reflections in this diary also serves as an open and continuing invitation for us all to stay present to ourselves, wherever we are, even as we bear in mind the deeper spiritual reality that enfolds us.

I hope that as we steadfastly seek to do this, we will do so not just in light of the so-called new reality brought on by our experience of the global pandemic. Even with the immediate and far-reaching repercussions of our current situation, we can aim to focus on the deeper, broader, and greater reality of our everyday life.

For the essence of our spiritual life, as we live it each day, is all-encompassing, regardless of the shifting conditions in which we find ourselves locally or abroad, in a monastery or in the marketplace, COVID-19 or no COVID-19.

At the crux of my seemingly endless struggle while in the abbey, I realized, was my utter inability to embrace the "sacrament of the present moment" (to borrow the title of Jean-Pierre de Caussade's classic work). My problem had mainly to do with my refusal to yield to God, in humble obedience, according to what and how God was summoning me to live: not from yesterday nor for tomorrow but within my today; not in faraway California but in the abbey in the southern Philippines, where God had placed me for a season (and for a purpose). I expended—and consequently wasted—a lot of energy trying to imagine what life had been and what it could be while glossing over what it simply was in the moment. It was my own loss that I did not allow myself to fully bloom where I was planted. By not being completely present where I was, I not only deprived myself but others as well, by often wishing I was somewhere else.

Now that I can look back and assess my plight at the abbey more objectively, I see how I embodied, for the most part, the exact opposite of the values of stability, obedience, and conversion I purported to promote. Because of my unwillingness to be where I was meant to be, I wrestled mightily with my own heart's stability while I was at the monastery. Moreover, I had a hard time responding to God in humble and willing obedience because I wasn't listening attentively to what God was doing in, through, and around me. There were times when I couldn't even be completely open to the abbot's suggestions and guidance because I was resistant inside.

Finally, I wasn't always truthfully open and welcoming to the inner work God was initiating, which was to move me toward my own ongoing renewal and conversion; instead, I was at times stubborn and hesitant to freely allow God to mold me and to work unhindered, in and through the thick of my situation, trusting in God's wisdom and good intentions.

Crucially, I know that I have not always been very present to God's presence every day and every moment. This was the most valuable and enduring lesson I acquired during my prolonged stay at the monastery.

Our life with God is truly a spirituality of everyday life, which is what constitutes the here and now as it is lived out in the chaos and tangle of our mundane existence. And, in fact, it's in the midst of all this—with or without the disruptive impact of a pandemic—that I can open myself up to experience and apply the ever-relevant core Benedictine values of stability, obedience, and conversion in my daily life—values that are admittedly a lot easier for me to profess than to express in more concrete ways.

Just the same, I have come to believe that the Benedictine ideals that promote the practice of everyday spirituality are not impossible pursuits for any of us. Neither are they the exclusive domain of monks and oblates. The life we each live every day in the present moment—in the ordinariness of it all—is the only normal life we can aim for, even when we stumble or fall.

As Benedictines are often fond of invoking, "Always we begin again!"

postface

I can hardly believe that almost six months have flown by since my departure from the abbey and my subsequent completion of this diary project. Nothing has changed dramatically; all of us still find ourselves living through a strange season, the end of which is anyone's best guess. Yet many of us have definitely moved on with life as it is—having no choice but to adapt to our present reality.

Here in Los Angeles, the situation has recently become even more challenging with the devastating wildfires that have hit closer to home (my wife and I came pretty close to evacuating our apartment in Arcadia at one point). The Bobcat fire even threatened to engulf Saint Andrew's Abbey in Valyermo, but thank God, it was miraculously spared after the monks evacuated the monastery.

All this has come about on the heels of our virtual closing residency retreat for our CenterQuest School of Spiritual Direction. It has been an equally challenging and stressful period for those of us directly involved in bringing our cohort 4 cycle to a close. The September 2 graduation celebration we had planned so meticulously to livestream was, from a strictly human standpoint, a technical disaster, reminiscent of the watch party snafu I hosted from the abbey last May (see May 9, pp. 189-190). Yet despite all the unexpected technological glitches we experienced during our residency retreat (which stretched from the original eight days to fourteen, given the time zone differences among the participants), the cohort 4 closing turned out to be very memorable. Indeed, there were plenty of reasons for us to celebrate another fruitful cycle, foremost of which was God's evident faithfulness in seeing us all the way through the process—mess and all.

Allow me to share with you some key updates on several fronts since I reentered life here in Southern California:

On the home front:

- After more than half a year of not seeing each other, our youngest son, David, who lives in San Francisco, visited us in August for a few days in Los Angeles. Juliet and I also enjoyed having him and his fiancée, Christy, for the Thanksgiving holiday last November. (David's wedding, originally set for last July 4, got postponed; see April 11, p. 100)

- Jonathan, our eldest—with whom I had a lengthy text exchange while I was at the abbey (see May 9, pp. 190-191)—seems to have slowly overcome his personal frustrations and found himself a new girlfriend (a Korean American from Atlanta). He has also embarked on a new line of work as a script coordinator with DreamWorks.

On the ministry front:

Since I returned from the abbey, I've been splitting my time working from home and from our CenterQuest office in Pasadena. Both my retreat and teaching ministries have predictably become fully remote and technology-driven:

- In July, I conducted my Henri Nouwen weekend retreat via Zoom for St. Benedict Center in Schuyler, Nebraska, with thirty-five participants in attendance. Immediately after that, I taught a weeklong Nouwen course (also via Zoom) for Vancouver School of Theology in British Columbia, Canada, with twenty-five students enrolled (see April 22, p. 135).

- I spent most of June, July, and a good part of August preparing for our cohort 4 virtual closing residency retreat and graduation, as well as processing applications and conducting Zoom interviews with a number of our cohort 5 applicants.

• After twelve years of working in my office in Pasadena (it started as the Nouwen Legacy Associates office until Center-Quest took it over in 2013), I had no choice but to give it up (I lost two of my sublessees sharing the office with me due to the pandemic). So, in the beginning preparations for cohort 5, I found myself right in the middle of a "moving experience" from mid-October to mid-November.

• Like I predicted, nine participants from our online Soul Companioning class last May (see May 24, p. 248) applied for our CenterQuest School of Spiritual Direction and were accepted into our upcoming cohort 5. Two from our July/August class and three from our August/September class also joined our cohort 5 lineup. All in all, we "harvested" a total of fourteen students for cohort 5, just from the last three consecutive introductory classes in spiritual direction—an unprecedented turnout and especially impressive considering the pandemic.

God knows how heavily I have invested my whole heart and soul into our cohort 5 recruitment. I've lost count how many prospective applicants I have engaged with in the past year—via text, email, phone, and Zoom calls—and now I see how the effort has paid off well beyond my expectations. This lengthy process was characterized by many alternating and sometimes even simultaneous experiences of disappointing losses and surprising gains—joy and grief, troubling questions and unexpected answers, dread and anticipation. When I survey our final cohort configuration, it's pretty humbling to realize that not everything has depended on my own vigorous recruitment efforts. Through the difficult but creative art of letting go, I've learned even better to cooperate with God, recognizing that ultimately it is God who handpicked each precious soul to comprise the communal journey that is now our cohort 5.

Now we're all in a state of intense preparation for this largest cohort to date, which is composed of thirty-four eager participants readying themselves for our virtual opening residency retreat in January 2021. Admittedly, we at CenterQuest are disappointed that we must once again gather virtually because of the restrictions imposed by the ongoing pandemic, which we can only hope and pray will soon come to an end.

At the same time, we're beyond ecstatic for all the wonderful momentum this new cohort is generating for us. This is by far the most diverse one we've ever had—*geographically* (from the United States, Canada, Australia, Mexico, Singapore, and the Philippines); *ecumenically* (Catholics—both lay and religious, Anglicans/Episcopalians, Methodists, Baptists, Pentecostals, evangelicals, and nondenominational Christians); *ethnically and culturally* (Southeast Asians [Filipinos and Singaporeans], Pacific Islanders [Australians], Asian Americans [Filipinos, Chinese, Korean, and Japanese], and other North Americans from Canada and the US); and even *age-and experience-wise* (from twenty-eight to eighty-five years old). We can't wait to partake in and celebrate this experience of diversity!

And finally, **on the abbey front**:
• Mark, the aspirant-observer with whom I went brisk-walking a couple of times, decided to join the abbey on June 13, 2020, and is now a postulant (see May 12, p. 199).

• St. Antony the Hermit Spiritual Center inaugurated its newly built chapel on July 11, 2020, coinciding with the Feast of St. Benedict, and is now officially open to retreatants (see April 1, p. 68).

• Abbot Ed was finally able to fly to Manila on August 7, 2020, to briefly visit his mother, whom he hadn't seen in person since February 2020, at the beginning of the pandemic (see April 19, p. 126).

• The Sunday Mass at the abbey church reopened its doors to the public on July 5, 2020, with social distancing measures in place, and has been livestreaming services via Facebook and YouTube to thousands of avid followers since September 13, 2020 (see March 29, p. 47).

On a more personal note, much as I wanted to settle the issue of my Catholic/Protestant identity struggle once and for all (see the Preface, pp. xvii-xviii;, April 13, pp. 108-109), I'm still unresolved and engaged in a continuing discernment process. It was very helpful for me, though, to have had the occasion of engaging Jon Sweeney (the editor in chief of Paraclete Press) in an enlightening phone conversation wherein he shared personal details of his own conversion journey from being an evangelical to an Episcopalian and finally settling to become a Catholic. There are many aspects in the lengthy process he went through to which I could relate. Our candid chat together was well worth it, even though the prospect of publishing the *Quest for the Center* book I've been working on with Paraclete Press ultimately didn't pan out (see March 26, pp. 36-37).

It surely would've been nice to arrive at some definite conclusion coinciding with this book's publication, but I don't feel compelled to rush into anything prematurely. This critical decision of mine inevitably implicates several arenas of my life and ministry in far-reaching ways. Thus I believe that it pays to wait, for however long it may take to arrive at the point where God's peace unquestionably reigns in my heart. For me, there will be no more turning back once I make up my mind about this issue.

In closing, let me offer this short meditation by Henri Nouwen, which I came across not too along ago. His vivid description of "a new vision of maturity" captures my own sentiments—both retrospectively, as I reflect back on my monastic interlude, and prospectively, as I press on to whatever lies before me. In view of my desire to keep fleshing out what a spirituality of everyday life may further mean for me, I welcome the perspective Nouwen offers here.

A New Vision of Maturity

I find myself with the same old struggles
every time I am in a new and unfamiliar milieu.
In particular,
the experience of isolation keeps returning,
not in a lessening but in an increasing degree.
Becoming older makes the experience of isolation much more
familiar—maybe simply because
of sheer repetition—but not less painful.

So maybe the question is not how to cope better,
but how slowly to allow my unchanging character to become
a way of humility and surrender to God.
As I recognize my fears of being left alone
and my desire for a sense of belonging,
I may gradually give up my attempts
to fill my loneliness and be ready
to recognize with my heart
that God is Emmanuel,
"God-with-us,"
and that I belong to him
before anything or anyone else.

And so a new vision of maturity may emerge;
not a vision in which I am more and more able
to deal with my own pains,
but one in which I am more willing
to let my Lord deal with them.
After all, maturation in a spiritual sense
is a growing willingness to stretch out my arms,
to have a belt put round me,
and to be led
where I would rather not go
(John 21:18).

Henri Nouwen
Daily Meditations

afterword

Wil Hernandez's thoughtful and warm-hearted diary of his unexpected two-month-stay at a Philippine Benedictine monastery has much to offer all of us who have found our lives unexpectedly interrupted by the coronavirus pandemic. Caught by the spread of the pandemic and its increasing health restrictions, Wil was forced to interrupt a projected schedule of retreat leadership while still maintaining his leadership and teaching at the Los Angeles–based CenterQuest School of Spiritual Direction, via virtual communication by way of a sometimes-inoperable internet linkage. He vividly describes thoughts and emotions so many of us have experienced in these pandemic times of uncertainty, through his much-magnified "season of divine interruption" (p. xxi).

Wil is by no means a novice in a structured spiritual life, having written four books and spoken internationally on the well-known Christian guide Henri Nouwen, and having himself been committed to life as an oblate in the Benedictine tradition for more than a decade. In his role as founder and executive director of CenterQuest, Wil spends many hours of each day pondering the relationships between and essence of spiritual disciplines, spiritual companioning, spiritual formation, and spiritual community. Even before entering this season of divine interruption, he had extensive resources and considerable experience in spiritual maturity. We might think that he, like the monastics with whom he spends time, would have had no difficulty maintaining a serene and wise presence, no matter what life throws at him.

The gift that Wil gives us in this diary is the gift of himself, "warts and all," as we say. Rather than pretending that he was able to slide serenely through all the challenges of this period, Wil offers himself honestly—exhausted, lonely, and impatient at times, troubled by necessary adaptations to mosquito-infested air, changing meal and sleep times, snake habitats, toothaches and periodic dizzy episodes, and sometimes the panicked sense that nothing is any longer in his control.

In the midst of all this, Wil also finds himself awestruck by the exquisite natural beauty around him. He finds that taking photographs is a soothing and sustaining practice that links him more closely to that beauty. Acquaintances notice and generously offer needed items, such as a warm jacket. Unexpected emails bring just the right word for the day. Sitting in on the daily communal prayer times, Wil moves from impatience with repetition to gradual awareness that he is being gently brought into "a personal homecoming of sorts—where scattered fragments of [his] broken self are slowly being integrated" (p. 55).

Wil realizes that, in fact, his emerging sense of wholeness is actually born "out of both inner and outer struggles so real that only genuine surrender can release their grip" on him. Bringing his own struggles to personal and communal prayer gives him the strength to let go (p. 55). The very rawness of the moment's difficulties opens him to a continuous broadening of his spiritual convictions (p. 262).

Seeking to summarize memories he will not forget, Wil finds himself cherishing the beloved peculiarities of each of the monks, who in their shared silence and occasional stories have revealed their own vulnerabilities and struggles.

And yet Wil tells us that his aim here is not so much to write about the monks nor about himself as rather to encourage us readers to stay present to ourselves, even and maybe especially when we are not particularly pleased with what we find, bearing in mind always the deeper spiritual reality that enfolds us (p. 263).

May we find his experience and his invitation welcome and healing.

Norvene Vest, PhD, Obl. OSB
Author, *Preferring Christ: A Devotional Commentary on the Rule of St. Benedict*
Editor, *Still Listening: New Horizons in Spiritual Direction*

www.composury.com

gratitude

W ere it not for the cooperation and support of Abbot Ed and the monks of the Abbey of the Transfiguration I would not have been able to complete this journal project within such a relatively short time. Thanks to all of you for your exceptional responsiveness to my endless texts, emails, and phone calls, and for supplying me with all the factual information I needed and more. I celebrate this timely completion with you all!

I am indebted to Daniel Harris for his personal investment into this project and for using his expertise in managing the publication process on my behalf. I knew I could count on Joel Dasalla, who designed the book covers for my trilogy on Henri Nouwen, to come through for me this time again—not just in doing the cover design but the overall layout of the book, which I really love to the hilt.

Nancy Lee Sayre, who also edited my Nouwen trilogy, attended to the initial editing of my rough manuscript and turned it into a much tighter, cleaner, and more cohesive version than it is now. Thanks, Nancy, for your thoughtful follow-up questions that forced me to clarify my own thinking and what I really wanted to convey more straightforwardly. Your suggested title for this journal won me over!

If there was one person who has expressed genuine belief in the potential of this project, it was Emily Wichland, my former editor for my fourth book on Nouwen with Skylight Paths Publishing. I have so appreciated our many phone conversations and the ways you have challenged and stretched my ideas for this book. Thanks for not just doing the final editing but for being there for me from the start to the finish. It was a joy to work with you!

Providentially, I stumbled upon Jerome Blanco, a *kababayan* (fellow Pinoy) now stationed in New York who, despite his tight schedule, agreed to do the final proofreading for this book. Thanks Jerome for patiently combing through the entire material. I really appreciate your last-minute assistance.

To my CenterQuest colleagues, most especially Lisa Myers (who serves as codirector with me for our School of Spiritual Direction [SSD]) and some members of our SSD Mentors Community (Linda H., Luisa, Madeline, Gerard, Cris, Carolyn, Margie, Marie, and Sr. M) as well as to a good number of my friends (both in the US and abroad)—too many to name here (you know who you are!)—who took the time to read early drafts of the journal and gave me invaluable feedback: many thanks to you and for your interest in this work.

Finally, I dedicate this chronicle to all of my Benedictine oblate friends worldwide, especially in the Philippines (Abbey of the Transfiguration in Malaybalay, Bukidnon; and Abbey of Our Lady of Montserrat in San Beda, Manila) and in the United States (Christ the King Priory in Schuyler, Nebraska; and Saint Andrew's Abbey in Valyermo, California). You all have been a part of my monastic adventure—directly or indirectly—through your prayers and encouragements. I have nothing but gratitude to God for allowing me to have this rare, unexpected interlude in my journey of being an accidental monk!

~~~

notes

27   *One of my favorite Benedictine authors*: Joan Chittister, "When Can We Not Quit?" *Vision and Viewpoint*, March 23, 2020; excerpted from *Songs of the Heart: Reflections on the Psalms* (New London, CT: Twenty-Third Publications, 2011), 94.

33-34   *Prayer of Thomas Merton: Thomas Merton, Thoughts in Solitude* (New York: Farrar, Straus and Giroux, 1999). Quoted in *Contemplative Monk* (blog), March 24, 2020, https://www.facebook.com/ContemplativeMonk/.

50   New York Times *headline*: Donald G. McNeil Jr., "The U.S. Now Leads the World in Confirmed Coronavirus Cases," *New York Times*, March 26, 2020.

54   Time *magazine article*: N. T. Wright, "Christianity Offers No Answers about the Coronavirus. It's Not Supposed To," *Time*, last updated March 29, 2020, https://time.com/5808495/coronavirus-christianity/.

54   *A poignant quote from the theologian and former archbishop of Canterbury*: Rowan Williams, quoted in *Contemplative Monk* (blog), March 31, 2020, https://www.facebook.com/ContemplativeMonk/.

54-55   *As if they weren't enough to chew on:* Joan Chittister, "An Audacity We Didn't Know We Had," *Vision and Viewpoint,* March 30, 2020; excerpted from *Scarred by Struggle, Transformed by Hope* (Grand Rapids, MI: Eerdmans, 2003), 19.

57-58   *"Indeed nothing is to be preferred":* Timothy Fry, OSB, ed., *RB 1980, The Rule of St. Benedict in English* (Collegeville, MN: Liturgical Press, 1982), 43:1, 19:1.

60   *"The spectacle we find in true religions":* Neil Postman, *Amusing Ourselves to Death: Public Discourse in the Age of Show Business* (New York: Penguin, 2005), 122.

75   *Courtesy of the Mystic Prayers site:* John O'Donohue, "For One Who Is Exhausted, a Blessing," Transmedia Service, September 28, 2020, https://www.transcend.org/tms/2020/09/for-one-who-is-exhausted-a-blessing/. Quoted in *Mystic Prayers* (blog), April 3, 2020, https://www.facebook.com/mysticprayers/.

99   *"At its core, contemplation is the practice of openness":* Reposted by David G. Benner, *Cascadia Living Wisdom* (blog), April, 2020. Original post, July 29, 2020, https://www.facebook.com/livingwisdomcascadia/.

136   *BBC News ran a thought-provoking news article:* "Coronavirus: World Risks 'Biblical' Famine Due to Pandemic—UN," BBC News, April 21, 2020, https://www.bbc.com/news/world-52373888.

138   *Today Christine excerpted this paragraph:* Christine Valters Paintner, *Illuminating the Way: Embracing the Wisdom of Monks and Mystics* (Notre Dame, IN: Sorin Books, 2016), 42.

171   *I remembered a couple of lines*: C. S. Lewis, *Till We Have Faces: A Myth Retold* (San Francisco, CA: HarperOne, 2017), 351.

175   *Right after posting my photo*: Craig Groeschel, *Life.Church* (blog). Quoted by *TobyMac* (blog), May 3, 2020, https://www.facebook.com/tobymac/.

219   *It's a beautiful day*: Quoted by *TobyMac* (blog), May 18, 2020, https://www.facebook.com/tobymac/.

272-224   *A line from the "Measure of the Fullness"*: Mark Beazley, "The Measure of Fullness," track 10 on *More Than My Words Can Say*, One Way Studios, 2016.

272-273   *In closing, let me offer this short meditation*: Henri Nouwen, "A New Vision of Maturity," Henri Nouwen Society, September 20, 2020, https://henrinouwen.org/meditation/a-new-vision-of-maturity/.

Center Quest

An Ecumenical Hub
for the Study and Practice
of Christian Spirituality

For more information,
check out

www.CQCenterQuest.org

or call

1-833-QUEST-05

Welcome
Cohort 5

The journey has begun...

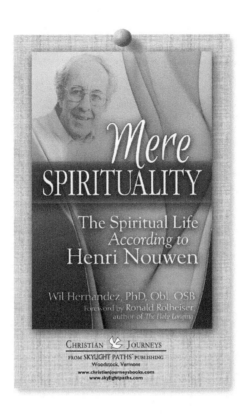

Also available:
Nouwen Trilogy from Paulist Press

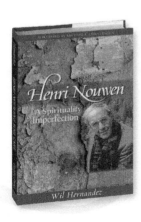

https://www.facebook.com/groups/915248668912670

Made in the USA
Middletown, DE
12 February 2021